PUSH DICK'S BUTTON

*A Conversation on Skating from a Good Part
of the Last Century—and a Little Tomfoolery*

by Dick Button

D0057463

ISBN: 1-4942-2347-3

ISBN-13: 978-1-4942-2347-2

To all the skaters that have brought the joy
of skating to so many.

CONTENTS

CONTENTS

ACKNOWLEDGMENTS

It seems I have always been lucky to have been blessed with great support from family, skating friends, and all those who have pushed and kicked me from behind to get this conversation finished. I cannot express my appreciation enough for all their help.

This conversation is one I have done myself but with so many helpful bits and pieces, thoughts, rusty hoots, information, and corrections that I feel it is not my work in any way. So if there are mistakes, they are mine. If anything is even more than just "OK," then it is due to their efforts and contributions.

My warmest thanks to:
Pat Eisemann, Benjamin Wright, Sonia Bianchetti, Lee Mimms, Edwin Cossitt, Alis McCurdy, Slavka Kohout Button, Doug Wilson, and last but certainly not least, Dennis Grimaldi

A NOTE TO READERS

Dear friends, neighbors and enthusiasts of the fine art of figure skating!

This is an invitation to come on over and join my dogs and me on my well-worn couch to watch the skating events on TV. I am inviting you to join a conversation on skating with a little schmoozing, some sound bites, and a few rusty hoots from a good part of the last century.

This is not a history of the sport of skating, nor is it a biography of me, nor is it a memoir. It's a conversation. Everyone likes a good conversation or story. I hope you will find some herein and that any questions you may have will be answered.

So come on in, climb up on my sofa, pat the dogs, and off we go!

Dick

COME ON IN, FOLKS!
THE DOOR'S OPEN!

If you look forward to watching national, world, or Olympic skating events, then please come and sit on the couch next to me and we will watch them together (I promise not to eat all the popcorn!) and we can talk about the many things of interest.

When it comes to watching skating, as the saying goes, it's all "in the eye of the beholder." One program excites us; another leaves us cold. But what exactly are we watching? An elite skater moves through a competitive routine at a pace so quick that the virtuosity on display (or not!) can be difficult to see, let alone consciously register and evaluate. Blink, and the move can be over.

That is why I am starting this conversation—to help guide you on what to watch. Forget the twirling fannies with their ruffles (if you can!). There are so many elements in skating that can capture your eye. But now that you are here on my couch and turning the TV on to the skating event, I would urge you to keep your eye on how the blade meets the ice, where you can see that an edge is a lean of the body, and then concentrate on everything that comes with it: the music, the costumes, the story that the skater is telling, and of course the points that are necessary in order to win.

Let's talk then about some of the elements that will make watching figure skating a little more understandable and fun. For example: what to look for in a skater's entrance . . . what centers a spin? . . . is there a jump in that jump? . . . costume delights and disasters . . . why there are no "figures" in figure skating . . . a "crash course" on the new rules . . . and lots more.

The history of skating over the last century is full of incidents both on and off ice that shed light on what might happen again at national, world, or Olympic events—incidents that are likely to surprise us, confuse us, or make us laugh—or that are so outrageous that they might blow our minds.

The last century? Good grief, are there any of us left from the 1948 Olympic Winter Games in St. Moritz or the 1952 Games in Oslo?

So remember, forewarned is forearmed!

There's still so much that needs to be clarified and explained, including for me, in this most unexplainable sport of all sports. Unexplainable because, in addition to requiring truly prodigious technical athletic ability, it also demands musical understanding, a sense of history, a feeling of space, a need for choreographic finesse, a concern for haute couture, and a full-blown awareness of what "performance" means.

For more years than I care to count, starting with CBS's coverage of the 1960 Olympic Winter Games in Squaw Valley (*you* do the counting!), I have been an on-air commentator for Olympic and World Championships and assorted other funny games for national TV.

The ostensible reason I was there was to guide the audience—"to comment"—on the finer points of the sport, which is why we were called, for better or for worse, "expert commentators"!

How did I get to this position? Easy! There was a vacuum.

The Olympics were new on television, and most sportscasters covering major sports were unlikely to be knowledgeable about figure skating and its rules. But I knew them intimately. Let's face it, friends on the couch, I had been a two-time Olympic gold medalist, five-time World Champion, seven-time U.S. Champion, and, most importantly, the runner-up in the Regional Subsectional Binman Avenue Juvenile Skating Jamboree.

I competed in my first skating competition at the tender age of thirteen, in the Novice event of the Eastern Figure Skating Championships in New Haven, Connecticut, in 1943. When I told the neighbors what I was doing, they asked, "What's a figure skating competition?" Certainly there wasn't any television coverage of the sport at that time. Skating was more or less an activity of folks who skated in the Skating Clubs like those in Boston, New York, and Philadelphia, and on outdoor ponds.

But when the 1960 Olympic Winter Games in Squaw Valley came around, television coverage had arrived. CBS bought the TV rights to those Games for $50,000. (Now they cost more than a billion dollars. Could there be any inflation here?)

At that time, it was necessary for a skating commentator (that was me, folks!) to point out the most basic moves. To the average viewer, an Axel was something on a car and a Salchow was just maybe a sick cow.

Today, audiences are inundated with detailed TV commentary, and endless information and opinions are everywhere on the Internet. Most viewers know a great deal about this sport, so these days it's less necessary to make commentary so basic (doesn't everyone know that a "flying camel" is not a camel that flies, but a "Button Camel"?). (A fuller explanation will be given later when we

3

have a drink at the bar.)

Figure skating, like everything else, has become much more complex. It might therefore be of some help for all of us to be guided through what can be one of the most complicated sports. I've always relied on experts to help guide me through stuff where I don't know as much as I think I know. *(Did I say that?)* That includes skating, where I still seek others' opinions on the rules, choreography, musical interpretation, technical merit, performance, costumes, and many other issues. (Correction! I try never to ask about the costumes of the ladies, because that can be a sinkhole of the most dangerous order.)

By researching the music, the skating rules, and the choreographic background, I understood why British ice dancers Jayne Torvill and Christopher Dean were so wildly successful when they competed in and won the ice dance competition at the 1984 Olympic Winter Games in Sarajevo. Their memorable performance to Maurice Ravel's *Bolero* received worldwide attention, was one of the most iconic ice dance programs ever, and changed the face of ice dancing.

But if Torvill and Dean had skated exactly the same program four years later at the 1988 Games, they would not have lasted five seconds—so changed, so controlling, so constipated had the rules become. In place of the freedom to create the choreographic concept called for by the music, heavy restrictions were quickly imposed: there was to be no kneeling on ice; no lying on the ice; official timing began when movement started, even if the skater had not moved a skate; and the music needed to have a clearer melody.

Hello??

Understanding the whys and wherefores of such changes gives us knowledge—The age-old saying, "Knowledge is power," should be counterbalanced by the other age-old saying, "A little knowledge is a dangerous thing." So I hope any comments I make herein will help give greater knowledge and understanding to the viewers of the skating events in the Olympic Games or elsewhere—and may also make me feel like the powerful, puffed-up, old Pooh-Bah that I have become in my doddering old age. (It is not necessary to say I was on my way a long time ago.)

Many times I received irate letters from fans saying I was spoiling their viewing of the skating programs by interjecting my critical comments. But after competing in, watching, dissecting, studying, examining, and researching the fine art of skating and taken on the job of commentating on it, I would have been remiss if I did not critique, explain, and try to guide the viewers.

Frank Carroll, the eminent coach of Olympic champion Evan Lysacek, Michelle Kwan, Linda Fratianne, and many other top skaters, has stated, "You don't know what it's like until you have been dissected by Dick Button on national television." I'm not sure whether that was as a result of my referring to him on TV as, "There's the old curmudgeon," but either way, my reputation was firmly established. The truth was that I only got excited about and criticized those skaters who I felt were talented. Honest criticism is born out of a fundamental passion. Honest criticism comes when you recognize talent in someone, and you want that person to experience the sheer joy of doing their best. Talented skaters are the ones who are interesting. So my reply would be, "You know I admire you if I criticize you!"

What I was attempting to provide was an understanding of a position, a point of view, a perception about an element in the choreography or a particular movement in a spin, on an edge, or in a jump. All of these contribute to the creative process that, ideally, results in a memorable performance.

And many times I made a mistake when calling some whippity-doo-dah jump combination. In this Internet age, everyone is knowledgeable and informed. Every statement you make can be criticized mercilessly.

But for anyone who thinks I may pull any punches out of fear of being criticized, let them beware! I've spent far too many years watching the Fine Art of Figure Skating and commenting on its wondrous idiosyncrasies to give a rusty hoot what anyone may think of my comments. Throw raw eggs at me if you like.

Unlike the ever-tactful Michelle Kwan (I'm sure I'll wake up one day to hear she's been appointed to a key diplomatic post), I would never last a minute as a diplomat.

But here's my little secret: I love all the epithets that have been tossed my way. Having been called so many imaginative, funny, and sometimes questionable things, I relish the opportunity to share them with you. Some of the best are:

Imperious Sage

Loudmouth

A comfortable old chair

A comic figure with alarmingly muscular legs

A combination of pedagogic schoolmarm and wildly enthusiastic fan

Popeye on Ice

Dispenser of "inane, insane, brilliance"

That eccentric, beloved, octogenarian, Ivy League skating professor

And some comments even I can't print. Skating is a family sport, after all!

So here we are: you who may once have been skaters (like me) and you, who may never have skated but who got hooked by the lure of this highly flamboyant sport, crammed together on this overstuffed coach with the striped slipcover that is reshaped by endless nights of dogs sleeping on it.

What is the lure of ice? For me it was the moment my brothers took me to Crystal Lake, a pond at the edge of Englewood, New Jersey that looked huge to my six-year-old eyes but that is now divided by Route 80 and much smaller. We also went to Coffin's Pond (at the foot of the wide lawn spreading down from forbidding nineteenth-century stone houses at the top of Palisade Avenue and right across from the Englewood School for Boys, which I was to attend years later).

What was it that kept us constantly hoping for cold weather and the "red ball" to go up over Crystal Lake? That was where entrepreneurial folks built a warming hut, charged 10 cents for skating and kept the "red ball" flag, a nineteenth-century signal that "the ice is ready" flying from a pole high enough for everyone to see (remember this tradition started in the nineteenth century when there were no telephones or internet, and visual signals were sometimes the best way to communicate).

Was it the cold that invigorated us? Was it the magic of being able to glide across the ice, "sculling" as my older brother George taught me (pulling my skates together and then pushing them apart, first forward and then backwards)?

Was it the ambiance created by music from a 78 record player broadcast over a tinny loudspeaker? The fire on the bank for warming our hands? The marshmallows someone brought, which we put on sticks and scorched in the fire? Was it the freedom of the moment or the pure joy of childhood that we didn't realize then was the pure joy of childhood?

Was it later the feeling of flying across ever-larger ponds with the wind behind us pushing us along, or the challenge of competition and its technical demands (as in: "I can do anything better than you can"—the idea behind the song that later was sung in Broadway's *Annie Get Your Gun*)? Was it the history of the Olympics (I think I knew every story by the time I was ten)? Was it the possibility of an ever-expanding selection of music available and allowable for competition, or the clothes that at first kept us warm or aided our ability to fly, and still later helped us complete the picture we were painting? Was it the theater of ice shows, the glamour and stardom of great skaters, and the fun of comics and vaudeville and even animal acts that had moved onto the ice? Was it the camaraderie of skating and then having Friday night dinner at the Skating Club? Was it the hypnotic flow of skating itself, the realization that "an edge is a lean of the body," or the exhilaration of being able to move without moving?

Is it the totality of this sport that grips us? The wildness of the costumes, or their elegance, and the things designers can do? Was it Vera Wang designing a white Grecian number for Nancy Kerrigan when she was famously whacked in the knee? Is it the extraordinary things the skaters can do and the enormous range of music that sweeps us along on flying blades—even though we may be glued to the couch?

I suspect that it's some of these things for all of us and all of these things for most of us.

Whatever it is is why we're all crammed together on this couch (maybe someone could push the dogs off? They won't listen to me!) where we are trying, but failing, to stop eating all the popcorn so quickly and impatiently waiting for the blasted commercials to end and the skating to start. So let's take first things first and prepare ourselves for what we will see even before anyone starts to fly over that slippery surface.

First: Look for quality of skating: how the skater moves across the ice, and the skater's edging (remember, an edge is created by a lean of the body).

Second: "Personality" should leap out at us.

Third: Expect the unexpected. The mystery of the judging will befuddle us. The specter of human drama and the misfortune of defeat will hover over all.

Fourth: Try to gain a sense of the rules. Easier said than done! Stay tuned for more in later chapters.

Fifth: Falls are to be expected. They can be fun and humorous but also dangerous and painful. I also hope to explain to you what, under the rules, a fall is—that is, if either you or I have the temerity to think we might know what a fall is in the first place.

Sixth: Expect change. I like to see the change that continually occurs in this sport and to the people in it. The way it develops from one generation to another. It's like the unruly child with raging hormones who acts up, goes wild, and almost falls overboard—and who then does something so magically different or throws a move that is so technically extraordinary or inventive that all you can do is wonder, "Could I do that?" and forgive every extravagance.

Damn this couch! I would much rather be half a century younger, flying over a glacier or a frozen surface behind the Palace Hotel in St. Moritz with the mountains as a backdrop, underneath the clearest blue sky, and where the cold didn't make you cold. But nowadays, talking about it and seeing it and watching the great history of this sport unfold in front of us is the next best thing.

It's easy to be able to see all this right here in my living room. When I was growing up, there was no television and no computers, and the only skating I could see was at the Palace Movie Theater in Englewood (down Palisade Avenue, across the train tracks, and to the right). When I heard something was showing that included skating, I paid my quarter and sat through whatever was playing, just to see the skating in the movie or the newsreel. Then I'd sit through the whole thing over again—the news that Sonja Henie's Hollywood Ice Revue was coming to New York City's Madison Square Garden, or a skating movie like *Sun Valley Serenade*, *Suspense*, or *One In a Million*.

I guess the things we get hooked on as kids can sometimes be the things that stick with us and remain a part of us forever.

So, will someone please make a whole mess of popcorn, open the nuts, and mix up a big bowl of guacamole? We need to fortify ourselves for what's to come tonight as we and the dogs sit too close on this comfortable old couch!

And we'll certainly sit here again soon, because there will always be skating enthusiasts who will want to see what Jim McKay on *Wide World of Sports* called "the thrill of victory and the agony of defeat."

1 ENTRANCES AND EXITS

Hey, the event is starting! Grab your beer, sit down and just squeeze in next to the dogs—by the way, the dog trying to climb into your lap is Cerrito, an Airedale. She's named after the mid-nineteenth century dancer Fanny Cerrito. Are you both settled in? Great! Now, let's all tune in to how skaters enter the scene.

Figure skating is theater and it always will be, even if the head honchos of the International Skating Union (ISU) have opted for it to be considered first, foremost, and almost exclusively a sport! And that, I am happy to puff up and say, is that! (When you get to be my age and you've seen as much of this delicious sport as I have, you can say anything you want. So there!)

Remember, even though this may be a national, world, Olympic, or any other high-stakes skating competition, it is still an activity that is set to music, enhanced by choreography and costumes, imbued with original thinking, and sparked by performance. And no matter whether some of the sports purists think it should not be in the Olympic Games, it is popular for just those reasons! That's why it has remained the most important and most-watched event of the Olympic Winter Games.

11

Which brings us to the first thing to notice in this most theatrical of sports: how do skaters enter the stage?

Did you ever have the opportunity to see one of the great dancers perform, such as Mikhail Baryshnikov, Rudolf Nureyev, Gene Kelly, Fred Astaire, Moira Shearer, or the extraordinary English ballerina Margot Fonteyn? Each was a master of the entrance and the exit (and pretty much everything in between).

When Margot Fonteyn entered the stage, she would float out from the wings and cross the stage as though she were tiptoeing on eggshells. She would pause for a nanosecond, then settle lightly into position. The conductor would raise his baton, the audience would hold its breath, the silence was complete . . . and the performance would begin.

Equally powerful were Nureyev and Baryshnikov. Each demanded your attention in his own way. Baryshnikov would burst on the stage like a fresh-faced schoolboy eager to show you what he could do. He was like a relaxed everyman, accessible and quiet, yet commanding. He was in control, informing you about the dance you were about to see. You became involved because of his mastery of steps, his animal-like movement, and his calm demeanor. You were not assaulted by his presence.

Nureyev, on the other hand, usually entered like an emperor: unapproachable, slightly threatening, as though expecting us to do obeisance. One was almost assaulted by his "put-off-ness." It seemed as if he might throw something at us if we weren't paying attention to "Himself." Of course, we were mesmerized.

So, how do skaters make their entrance? In fact, their entrance begins long before they step onto the ice to perform. How do they enter the arena building (which the television crew always covers)? How do they stretch and warm up off-ice, on a mat or elsewhere? How do they conduct themselves during the on-ice warm-up?

What is their starting position? How do they begin their program? At what point do they enter the character they may be playing or let the effect of the music they have chosen take over?

I believe you can always tell a skater's mood and confidence instantly. You can see whether they will be controlled and on a calm path or overwhelmed by the moment, susceptible to nerves, and potentially headed for disaster. Determine for yourself if the skater feels the theatrical essence of the moment and makes use of it or ignores it and then has to catch up in bringing the audience into his or her sphere.

Watch each skater, pair, or dance couple as they make their entrance and begin their program. Then go ahead and smile, become mesmerized, start cheering, or hold your breath at whatever you may or may not see in the next few minutes.

Each skater will treat his or her entrance differently. I know that it's a nerve-wracking time of great tension. After all, they've worked and trained hard for this for years. And this is it! Take a look at what they're telegraphing to the thousands in the arena, to the judges, and to the millions watching at home—including our happy little horde on this couch.

I shouldn't be mouthing off about how the entrance affects others without first saying how it affected me. I remember how I felt sitting in the dressing room in Davos, Switzerland at the 1948 World Championship, my second World Championship. I was waiting to be called to start and I felt a knife start turning in my stomach. I was cringing at the thought of having to step on the ice. I remember saying over and over to myself, "I don't have to do this. I don't need this."

After what felt like forever, my name was called and I took the long walk to the ice. I left my skate guards by the entrance, felt the cold air, and saw the grey sky over the huge skating surface sitting under the towering sides of the

13

Parsenn and Jacobshorn slopes that framed Davos. I looked over and saw the nine judges sitting in chairs right on the ice. They were wrapped in heavy coats, hats, gloves, and huge straw boots. Remember, this was outdoors, not in a warm arena, and they knew it would get very cold watching twenty-odd competitors skate their five-minute programs.

I took my starting position and breathed deeply. The music began (it was *Roumanian Fantasy*, orchestrated by Andre Kostelanetz). Something in me stirred, and the leaden weight I'd felt in my arms and legs disappeared. I gained confidence and quickly loosened up with each step. My head got into the game!

A totally different situation occurred two years later at the 1950 World Championships, in Wembley Arena in London. In the dressing room, I chewed gum to keep my mouth from going dry. I never skated a program with gum in my mouth because I would inevitably have swallowed it. But when my name was called and I skated out to center ice, I realized I had forgotten to remove it! Instead of beginning my program, I raised my hand to signify "not ready," skated over to the hockey barrier, and stuck the gum on it. I didn't mean it to be insulting or in bad taste, but the newspapers had a field day with it. The headlines the next day read, "World Champion Sticks His Gum on the Judges' Stand." It was an entrance that clearly did not support the creative concept of the program, but it did get the attention of the audience.

Remember the "Battle of the Carmens" when Katarina Witt and Debi Thomas both selected music from Georges Bizet's opera *Carmen* for the Long Program at the 1988 Olympics in Calgary, and sparks flew? It was much like two high-powered ladies each showing up at a party wearing the same dress.

The "Battle" was the subject of an almost crazed interest by the press. And why not? It featured two great-looking ladies, and both were great athletes. They were from countries politically and economically opposed with a long history of antagonism (Debi was African-American; Katarina East German). There were still undertones of World Wars I and II and the 1936 Olympics in Berlin where Jesse Owens was the centerpiece of Hitlerian hostility.

Katarina and Debi held the top two spots after the Compulsory Figures and the Short Program. The Long Program would decide who got the gold medal.

When Katarina skated out, she was wearing a red and black dress that reeked of Carmen and a wicked smile that exuded sexuality and complete confidence. She skated without mistakes.

Debi came out in a black costume with glittery decoration. She stood at the hockey barrier with her coach, Alex McGowan, who had been miked up by the television crew so that the whole world (which, believe me, was watching) could listen to his breathless last-minute instructions. He was holding Debi's hands, making the most of what was clearly his fifteen seconds of fame. It seemed to me that his instructions were insistent and continuous. Finally they slapped palms in a "low five," and she skated to center ice. From what I could see, she had little sense of calm.

All during Debi's program, Katarina stood at the rink side. Her red dress, red lipstick, darkened eyes, and focused stare drilled into her rival.

Debi made a mistake. Katarina won.

Whether their entrances contributed to the outcome of the competition or not, I will never know. But they made an indelible impression on me. Watching body movements and honest reactions on the skater's face can tell you a lot!

The Russian skater and World Champion Irina Slutskaya was a teenager in every sense, with the most perfect apple cheeks I have seen. I asked her once during an interview if I could pinch her cheeks. "Oh yes," she told me, smiling. "All the old men like to pinch my cheeks!" (I probably shouldn't, wouldn't and couldn't ask this today, but her answer was perfect—and besides, I like telling this story.) When her moment came, she would enter through the half door in the hockey barrier and skate over to her coach, Zhanna Gromova. Then, in front of some 20,000 in the arena and untold millions watching on television, she would blow her nose! Once finished, she'd adjust her dress (and her pants, too). Then she would listen to her coach! (What could her coach possibly tell her at this point that she hadn't already heard?) Finally, she'd take a swig of water and move out to the center ice to take her starting position. But instead of starting, she'd skate around with neither tension nor stretch in her body and with rounded shoulders, looking down. What was she looking for? A four-leaf clover, frozen in the ice? Head still down, she'd slowly search for a place to begin, find it, then raise her arms into a starting pose, and, lo and behold, smile!

Now, this was certainly not a humdinger of an entrance! It was not one that gave the audience a sense of anticipation, and she then had to work overtime to get the audience involved. So often in a warm-up, we see skaters in full costume skate around, wiggle a bit, pretend to test the ice or make a pseudo pull-up of the arms as though they're pretending to warm up with an Axel or a waltz jump, and then finally take a position. No dancer worth his or her salt would pull such movements before the start of a performance!

Sonja Henie, the three-time Norwegian Olympic Champion in 1928, 1932, and 1936, became an iconic show skater and movie star. She would have known exactly what to do to wring the maximum effect from her entrance, swinging her blond curls in a most delicious "Norwegian Skating Doll" style, or visibly touching the diamond pin at her throat.

Katarina Witt also knew the value of a theatrical

entrance. At the 1984 Olympic Winter Games in Sarajevo, she stood at the side of the rink knowing that not only every man in the audience was watching her, but every woman, too. Her coach, Jutta Müller, stood next to her talking to her, but Katarina clearly was not listening. Instead, she gave a most feminine pat to her hair, exuding confidence and sexuality, and looking like she'd been budgeted with a trillion dollars with no sequester in sight; skated out and instantly took her place, challenging us not to look at her.

I've always admired the class and restraint of the entrances of British ice dancers Jayne Torvill and Christopher Dean.

In their historic 1984 Olympic performance set to Maurice Ravel's *Bolero*, they calmly skated to center ice and took their position, never giving a single ounce of recognition to the expectant audience. They made it seem like they were not performing for anyone other than themselves. In their incredible and iconic presentation of *Bolero*, it was the rules that shaped their start. The program clock started when they started skating. In order to stay within the time limits and not have to cut the music, they simply kneeled on the ice and we the audience became voyeurs as they, weaving and bobbing, signified their attraction to each other and began the web that bound us in their grasp.

Then there was American Janet Lynn, the 1972 Olympic competitor who would stand patiently in her starting position. One could see calmness in her slow, deep breathing as she quietly prepared to hear the music. Invariably she'd break into the slightest of smiles that for us signified her joy in skating. We were mesmerized.

Canadian Toller Cranston, World and 1977 Olympic medalist, skated with the most stretched and extended body I have ever seen. He once did an exhibition program to the music of *Pagliacci* by Ruggero Leoncavallo. Playing the clown, he skated out to the center of the ice in full clown costume and crouched down on one knee, waiting for the famous cry to begin. The audience was silent. In the arena nothing stirred. But as the famous cry descended, some lady in the audience who did not know the opera or the music or the way he had edited it for the program, burst out laughing. Toller held his position and ignored the laughter, letting the piercing scream in the music take hold. The program began. He skated the role clearly and with conviction. It was an unforgettable display of control and concentration, and the audience was transfixed.

In 2011 we all went to the Adirondacks when the Skating Club of Lake Placid honored Oleg Protopopov and Ludmila Belousova for their lifetime dedication to skating. They were the first pair in the Russian juggernaut of skaters who dominated both Ice Dancing and Pair Skating, starting in 1964. Oleg and Ludmila have inspired skaters and audiences for over half a century. They survived defection from Russia and still maintain rigorous daily practices. They were, as usual, in fine fettle.

Their performance was held in the 1980 Olympic Arena that had some 15,000 seats that were mostly empty. The evening had not been well advertised. But a small group of admirers were there. The Protopopovs performed as though the arena was full and we, the audience, were the Royal Family. Skating has always been their oxygen!

Their opening position was all one needed to see to understand their artistry. The perfection of their line, the stretch of the leg ending in a pointed toe, and the stance of their bodies told the whole story, even before they started to move.

Remember, all of this is necessary in the quest for a medal. Ultimately, that medal is most valued when a skater has done the very best that skater can do at that very moment.

Passions between competitors can run high and rivalries abound. Who can forget when Tonya Harding was involved in a conspiracy to have rival Nancy Kerrigan whacked in the knee at the 1994 U.S. Championships in Detroit? So I hope you can imagine what's at stake in those moments as you see the skaters step onto the ice!

Listen, folks, the theater doesn't end with the last toe pick or position. It should and does encompass a curtain call. I urge you to watch the way skaters exit their performance. You've watched the entire performance. Maybe it was highly dramatic. Perhaps the concept of the program, its choreography, costume, and quality of performance were meticulously prepared. You may have your own opinion of how they performed, but far too many skaters let you know exactly how they think they skated. Does that in turn influence the judges? It certainly influences us sitting here on this couch! We can see on their faces if they did or didn't do well; if they landed (or didn't land) a "quadruple" (that jump with four revolutions, popularly known as a "quad"). How many times have we seen a skater grimace in frustration? And why would they, as performers and competitors, let the audience, not to mention the judges, know their frustration?

Recently, we've seen many a skater pump the air with their fists in exultation or kneel down and kiss the ice. Once, an over-enthusiastic entrant started knocking knees together like a wide receiver when he catches a pass and scores a touchdown.

What is this?

Football players spend months perfecting a play. But a skating program is not that kind of play; rather, it might be a performance set to "Nessun Dorma" from Puccini's opera *Turandot*. A performance like that is embellished with great music, thought-out choreography, costuming, and makeup. Some sort of acknowledgment is welcome and may be needed at the end of such an undertaking, but it's not the fist pump you see on a football field. We don't see fist pumps at the end of *Swan Lake* at the theater. So maybe they should not be seen at the end of a *Swan Lake* skating program. Fist pumping takes the "performance" out of the "performer" and the audience out of the performance.

Too many skaters forget this. High jinks like knocking knees and fist pumps reflect a different set of rules. This behavior may be acceptable to those who insist that figure skating is only a sport, but not to me. Even though figure skating, like speed skating, hockey, and skiing, must be judged on speed, strength, and number of revolutions (the figure skating equivalent of whether the puck lands in the net), it still also needs to be judged on creative elements. Figure skating is a sport where it doesn't always matter how fast you finish your program, but *how* you finish it. Besides, fist pumping or kneeling and kissing the ice has been done too many times to be funny, original, or anything other than boring. Think out of the box, guys and gals, and show us some subtlety and imagination.

As long as I'm on this mini-rant, let me say that another "watch for" is that too many skaters end their program by just falling off their final position. Flop! Flop! Plop! *Not!* A "floppy finish" doesn't complete the painting. It robs the audience of seeing the finished piece of art.

To see what I think is an impressive exit, log onto the Internet and watch a video of Peggy Fleming in Philadelphia in 1968, giving an exhibition program to *Ave Maria.* Her final position, when she descends to one knee, stretches the other leg and foot behind her, and carefully and slowly extends an arm forward, holding that last position for what seems like an eternity, is exquisite. It was one of the most satisfying elements in an otherwise fully satisfying performance.

Am I getting to be too conservative? Have I forgotten sticking my gum on the judges' stand and all the other shenanigans we did as young Turks? (So, throw the mustard at me). Am I hopelessly out of touch with today's culture, where everything is two seconds long; where fist pumps can be either up and stabbing the air like a drunken cowboy or down like the moves of a straphanger on a jerking subway ride? Am I fighting futilely against the world of today where you can twitter, tweet, or toot in Timbuktu and everyone will know it; where anything can go and frequently does?

Well, let me tell you an aside (as you might already have guessed, I do a lot of these) that is really far off-center. I once co-produced a play on Broadway called *Artist Descending a Staircase* by Tom Stoppard. I always liked his writing and remembered a quotation from another play of his entitled *Rosecrantz and Guildenstern Are Dead*. He wrote: "We do on stage things that are supposed to happen off, which is a kind of integrity if you look at every exit as an entrance somewhere else."

So, if we look at the exit of a skating performance, which has been structured as a creative performance, as maybe a re-entrance from the world of theater back into our crazy world, maybe a little fist-pumping is OK! Even though I'm a stubborn old curmudgeon, I can still understand the reasons for opposing arguments. Both might have value! So . . . my earlier point is also right. And by the way, didn't the National Football League (NFL) curtail excessive end zone celebrations and touchdown theatrics a while back?

Bottom line: I believe there is little place for shallow flash right at the end of a performance. Every style of music and movement, whether classical, jazz, hip-hop, or whatever, has its own look. Each position, each concept, each move must be thought out and considered. A skater should hold that last position, take a breath, and show the audience, the judges, and you and me, that they have completed the picture they were painting and are proud of it!

(Now, try to tell the judges how to mark that extra quality!)

2 BOOTS, LACES, AND POINTED TOES

Skating is dancing on ice! Skaters and dancers are like "kissing cousins." They have much in common. Both perform to music. Both use choreography to lie out the sequence of their moves. Both need "passion" to enhance there dance or program. Both have athletic demands and tensions. Both communicate a story or an idea, whether it is something traditional like *Swan Lake* or abstract like a Jackson Pollock painting.

Both are a form of personal expression. Personal expression requires thought.

But skating and dancing have differences. Skaters can move without moving. They can push off onto one foot, take a position, and sustain it while flying around the rink. A dancer, on the other hand, cannot "glide" anywhere.

Skaters have the Olympic games, which can catapult them to instant fame. There are no Olympic medals in dance. Therefore a dancer, even an extraordinary one, needs an opportunity either to defect from an unrelenting country (remember the days of the Soviet Union, when defectors took their life in their hands), or to make a movie, star in a Broadway musical, or perform for years to establish a reputation that still may never enter into the general public's consciousness.

But skaters have disadvantages that a dancer doesn't have. They wear a skate, which on the positive side allows for the reduction of friction and gives them freedom of speed and the ability to fly. But the skates have to be attached to a boot—and that's where an unattractive element can rear its ugly head and mar the overall look of a skater's performance.

Sonja Henie in the 1920s was the first to wear white instead of black boots. Believe me, that was a major innovation, and every lady skater after her made the change, too. Today, some of the ladies choose tan leather rather than white, which can be attractive. Some pull their flesh-colored, full-length tights over their boots to keep an uninterrupted color and therefore give a longer look to the leg.

Others—and I detest this!—fail to tuck their shoelaces into the top of the boot. The loose ends of the laces flopping about arrest the eye and call attention to the boot instead of allowing one to concentrate on the movement of the whole body. Tuck them in! It takes little effort (if I could do it, anyone can do it!), and there's too much riding on every performance to ignore this.

To the many lady skaters who wear white boots: why not at least make sure they're clean and sparkling white? Too many leave their boots looking like they've been washed in dirty water or been worn when composting the vegetable garden. In addition, the heels should be stained dark and kept crisp looking. In my day, diligent parents were frequently seen sanding the white leather to remove spots and then carefully applying dark lacquer to the soles and heels to show the contrast. It made the skaters look spiffy. There is no way to know if the judges notice this, but I do.

For me, flopping laces and dirty boots signify carelessness, thoughtlessness, laziness, or stupidity.

OK, I've said it, and I'm glad.

And another rant: Those skaters (both male and female) who are conscious of pointing their feet are the most aware of the importance of the line of the body. Olympic diving champion Greg Louganis instinctively performed with stretched legs that were locked tight together and always with feet and toes fully pointed. If divers didn't do that, they'd never make it to the medal stand!

Now, don't tell me diving is not figure skating! The principle of creating the longest possible line with the body is the same, and while it's harder to achieve the effect with boots on, it's still the effect to strive for.

Many skaters are "big boned" (translation: muscular) or are "heavy" jumpers like Brian Boitano or myself. Many skaters prefer very strong leather in their boots, which can feel and sometimes act like steel boot constructions. These support the landing of long, multiple-revolution jumps that need to land cleanly on steady edges on the narrowest of blades. Strong boot strength can provide confidence in that.

Some skaters can't or don't try to point their toes. Others are like John Curry, who always kept his boots loose and well-worn so he could achieve a "dancer's line" (admittedly he did not do quadruples). Paul Wylie, Johnny Weir, Patrick Chan, and others achieve a semblance of pointed feet. The goal is to keep the foot from being "obvious" and calling attention to itself. The best skaters have a straight back and stretched legs and feet in a streamlined, unified whole. Many pair skaters do a death spiral where the lady's foot is high in the air, sticking up like a sore thumb (ugh!).

I inherited the skates of the famed German skater "Charlotte." Her full name was Charlotte Oelschlagel, but a simple Charlotte was sufficient. She predated Sonja Henie. Charlotte came to America as early as 1915 and starred in Charles Dillingham's theatrical extravaganzas at the Hippodrome in New York City, and in movies like *I*

Spy and *Flirting in St. Moritz.* She is best known today as the inventor of the "Charlotte Stop."

For skating nutcases like us, a "Charlotte Stop" is a back spiral or "arabesque" on one foot with the free leg as high and straight up as possible and the head down and close to the skating foot so the two legs are in as much of a full split position as possible. The "stop" happens when the skater allows the skate to rise to the toe pick and comes to a complete stop while still holding the full vertical split position.

(As an aside, note the superb "Charlotte Stop" performed by Sasha Cohen, which she frequently performed and which became an eye-popping signature move in her program. Remember, it's not just about what we see, but that what we see should *register.*)

(And as still another aside: the "free leg" is the leg you are not skating on. It's therefore "free" from supporting you and free to put in any old cockamamie position. Like the one in a "Charlotte Stop" or even in a Biellmann spin, which is a story we'll get into later!)

Charlotte's skates were made of the softest, silvered, glove leather, with ballet toe-shoe openings between each hook. She was a powerful lady of substantial physique and did difficult jumps, but always remained conscious of her feet.

One means of affecting pointed feet so they don't look like clubs, even if you're wearing steel-strength boots, is to "turn out" the foot. This means to point the toes as much as possible and then rotate in the hip to turn the leg open and to the side as much as possible, and when stretching the leg behind, turning the foot flat to the ice or up away from the ice. This takes the viewer's eye away from what might otherwise look like the wooden head of an old-fashioned golf club.

Peggy Fleming often did moves in front of a mirror. She thus was able to check every turn, edge, and line, as well as her arm, leg, and foot positions. Most rinks have

26

large mirrors for this purpose. The point is, if skaters see and then register the ugliness of unpointed feet or any other detracting body positions, they can and will find ways to solve the problem.

The desire to see an elegant line, I might add, is a personal fetish on my part. I doubt if it would mean any more or less points under the current judging system.

The subject of body position will be touched upon later while we wait for a new batch of popcorn to pop.

And since I seem to be addicted to asides, let me here remind parents of skaters just starting out that strong, snug boots are essential to give a sense of security to young skaters as well as to the Brian Boitanos of this world who are powerful jumpers. The cry of "I have weak ankles" is one that would easily be squelched if parents did not buy skates that were too large, needing multiple layers of socks, with the idea of allowing the youngster to "grow into" them. It is necessary to buy boots that fit *now*, and you don't necessarily have to wear heavy socks for support. Thin socks can also help in feeling your connection to the edge and to the ice. Remember, you are balancing on a slim blade!

If fathers are buying, they should remember how easy it is to turn one's own ankle even when wearing a wide, size 12 shoe and buy boots that aren't loose. And mothers should recall their attempts to look like a cutey-pie while tippy-toeing on stilettos.

3 WHERE ARE YOU WHEN WE NEED YOU KATARINA WITT?

Dear friends and neighbors, can I tell you that over the course of almost three quarters of a century I have witnessed some pretty delicious moments in costuming? (Well, maybe delicious is the wrong word!)

The traditional feeling regarding skating programs is that the music, the choreography, and the costume should all support the creative concept. Each should support the whole, and it is most satisfying when this occurs.

But what we see first is what the skater is wearing, and believe me, we have seen everything from beaded and torn skirts to tassels, flounces, feathers, and even military knockouts. No other sport pays this much attention to what an athlete wears, so maybe it's time to chat about what skaters wear in their performances.

I've seen skating outfits that were simple. The dress Peggy Fleming wore when she won the 1968 Olympic Winter Games in Grenoble was made by her mother. Peggy had to stand for hours on a box while it was pinned and pinned some more, and then stitched together. It was a plain, long-sleeved, high-necked dress. The color was chartreuse, chosen by her mother because Grenoble was in the middle of the region where the Chartreuse liqueur had been created by Carthusian monks and was a favorite of all. The dress was understated and elegant, to say the least.

Sometimes skating clothes can go over the top and be so distracting that they can dull your eyesight. There is a young Russian skater named Elena Radionova, who is fourteen and may be too young to make the Olympic team this winter. She is a long-legged, perky, exuberant, jumping phenomenon with the tight and pointed feet in her jumps. The costume she wore for the Free Skate at Skate America (where she placed third) and for the NHK Trophy in Japan (where she came in second) was enough to make you wonder if she was a fugitive from one of the worst of the child beauty pageants. It had beading everywhere; long, decorated gloves; fringe; bare midriff; and a rhinestone necklace that would have choked Kim Kardashian.

Let's look back a bit—even though a little history can be a dangerous thing! Back in the dark ages of my day, it was expected that men would wear coats and ties when skating (which could be cumbersome and restrictive). Women would frequently be dressed in outfits that had what I learned were called "princess necklines." (Now there's a fascinating fact!) From there, things went downhill. For men, shoulder pads and a black tie look was the norm. There's even a picture of me in black tights, black coat, and a white stock shirtfront, which I refuse to show, no matter how much you beg!

It was a blessing then when Gustave Lussi, my teacher and a major force in the skating world, gave me a cardigan jacket. He had worn it much earlier in the 1920s. It was made of woven material like a sweater (no shoulder pads!). It was soft and molded to the body. It had a woven belt and was worn over black pants. It was, for me, a refreshing break from the restrictive norm.

It also worked because I was able to use it in the 1948 Winter Olympic Games in St. Moritz, where the free skating was held outdoors in the afternoon light in an outdoor stadium. ("Stadium" seems a generous term for the rink, which was sited on a small, snow-covered hill with some 5,000 seats on one side only just down from the Kulm Hotel. Compare that with the mega-rinks at the Olympics today!)

A black costume stood out against a background of white snow and in the shifting afternoon light. Mountain light could be bright and change rapidly from bright moments to lighter ones or to streaks of sunlight or to grey when a cloud passed over or the sun went down over the mountains, or when any number of things happened.

The previous year, the 1947 World Championships in Stockholm had been held outdoors, but at night. There were few lights on the ice. It was 1947 and the economic ravages of WWII were still everywhere. I made the decision to wear a short, white mess jacket. Such a break with tradition was necessary in order to be seen in an almost black setting.

It caused a furor.

I had seen this uniform in Navy mess jackets worn in the summer. However, the number of criticisms as to taste, such as, "Does he think he's a waiter?" were many, and some were vehement.

The next year, many skaters elected to wear similar white jackets, but by then the ruckus had subsided.

A ruckus? For Pete's sake! But remember, ridiculously insignificant things can cause a ruckus in the sensitive world of figure skating.

At the time, the coming revolution in stretch fabric and the psychedelic world of the sixties was still more than a decade away. Then our eyes would be assaulted by the imaginative inspirations of many skaters and by some of the most extravagant and over-the-top costume concoctions I had ever seen.

In the 1980s, Katarina Witt, the East German Olympic Gold Medalist, frequently appeared in costumes that could knock your eye out. At the 1984 Olympics in Sarajevo, she skated in a fetching powder blue costume crisscrossed with sequins dotted with powder puffs and sporting feathered highlights. The costumes she wore were always dazzling, even if sometimes reminiscent of a nightclub act, and this one was no different. The problem was not that her costumes sometimes resembled Las Vegas at its best, but that one of them was *very* skimpy.

Katarina's costumes made a major impact. Even "Dr. Ruth" (Westheimer), who earned fame as one of America's most popular sex therapists and television personalities, reported in her marvelous, slightly "strudel-like" accent that "Katarina should avoid sexy costumes that could arouse the judges" and that maybe there "should be some regulations on what kind of dress is appropriate."

Thank heaven the children are in bed! (They aren't. They're watching and listening to everything from the landing at the top of the stairs!)

At any rate, the Technical Committee, the rule-making arm of the International Skating Union (ISU), had its microscope out and instantly pounced. It seems that too often folks in power are not considered to be in power unless they are exercising that power. Rule makers aren't rule makers unless they are making rules (in the skating world as well as in Washington).

Forgive me for another aside (here I go again) for whatever underlying reason—but maybe also because one of the powder blue powder puffs was too strategically placed for the taste of the Technical Committee—*voilà*! So what was already known among all us serfs now became known to the hoi polloi as "The Katarina Witt Rule for Young Ladies of Gentle Birth and Upbringing." (The actual name was Rule #500, but why spoil a good story with the truth?)

Like the creation of the Sarbanes-Oxley act or the removal of the gold standard, the skating world was now supposedly cleansed and placed on the right path for young minds to emulate. Interestingly, later on, when Katarina popped out of her dress in a camel spin, there was not another rule amendment—perhaps because that was a legitimate (?) malfunction! Besides, the rule was already established. (Regrettably!)

For anyone who remembers the ice dancing competition in the 2002 World Championships, do you recall the "double pop-out" that occurred throughout the program of the skater in white (and it wasn't the guy!)?

I wonder how the Technical Committee would ever have written a rule that penalized a skater for permitting her Strategic Extravagances to pop out, or to cover the concept of nudity? When the Committee wrote "the Katarina Witt Rule" (now Rule #500), there must have been many questions they would have asked. Imagine what they'd have had to ask to come up with a Strategic Extravagances Rule! Exactly what was the Strategic Extravagance that popped out? How far did whatever popped out pop out? How much was exposed? And how much was there to be exposed? Was it elaborately adorned with jewelry (remember Janet Jackson's famous "wardrobe malfunction" at the Super Bowl)? How many points would be deducted, and would everything be measured as in speed skating—based on what crossed the line first? How much nudity would it take to be defined as nudity?

I can just see the debate (if there was one) over this!

My question is, why was a rule like "the Katarina Witt Rule" necessary in the first place? If the judges had disapproved of the costume, the nudity (or anything else), couldn't they have just voted their disapproval? Could the Technical Committee have been neither fashion- or show biz-conscious, or was their funny bone bent out of shape? Or did they sniff and snort at the sight of something even slightly suggestive?

Good grief! Why not give the judges some credit for being able to make intelligent decisions of their own?

And while I'm at it, isn't it about time we recognized what's in front of our eyes? Instead of sniffling and snuffling about costumes that are too skimpy, let's remember that the human body has been celebrated forever. Do you expect that if you take your children to Europe, you'll avoid going to the Louvre in Paris to see the Venus de Milo or the Winged Victory, even though they may have lost some parts in the intervening years? And what about a trip to the Accademia di Belle Arti in Florence to see Michelangelo's David? What about allowing them to use a computer where, even with parental controls, they can access everything? What about letting them stop by any newspaper store?

Back a ways, when many wild spirits were "streaking," Caroline Lussi, the daughter-in-law of skating coach Gustave Lussi, was skiing with her young daughter when another skier sans anything but ski boots went streaking past them down the mountain. It happened too fast for anything to be done other than to close up one's jaw that had dropped wide open.

Caroline waited to see and hear what her daughter would say. She finally turned to her mother and said, "That must be cold!"

And let's not forget when *Playboy* published a series on Katarina Witt in the altogether. It sold a record-breaking number of copies, offended no one that I heard of, was forgotten by some, remembered by many, and we all moved on.

Skating doesn't need more rules. A camel (the animal, not the skating move), it has always been said, looks like it does because it was designed by a committee. We should allow the judges to assess the realm of costumes as part of the performance, use their common sense, and decide for themselves.

I would have given low marks for some of the wild extravaganzas we've seen over the past decades, not for their skimpiness but for their truly ugly look. But I would have defended forever the skaters' right to experiment, to explore new directions, and to think outside the box.

For example, I would not have rewarded with points (but still had the best time seeing) the costumes worn by the Ukrainian ice dancers Elena Grushina and Ruslan Goncharov at the 2006 Winter Olympics in Torino. She wore tassels in two strategic places and seemed capable of getting them both to twirl at the same time but in opposite directions.

Shades of Minsky's Burlesque! Shades, too, of the musical *Gypsy*, based on the life of burlesque's biggest star, Gypsy Rose Lee. I met Gypsy through Paul Feigay, my partner in Candid Productions and a Broadway producer (*On the Town*) who had been a creative force behind the innovative CBS TV program *Omnibus*. Gypsy lived a block away from me on East 63rd Street in New York City, so I got to know her well. One of the songs in the musical was "You Gotta Have a Gimmick" (lyrics by Stephen Sondheim). Could this have been the inspiration for the tassel-twirling ice dancer's costume?

Now, if you want to hear another beauty, recall the time when the Technical Committee issued instructions regarding lifts that it deemed were too suggestive. The whole brouhaha was about the upside down (and other positioned) moves that were appearing in both pair and ice dancing events. Charlie Cyr, an official of United States Figure Skating (USFS) and an international ice dance judge, was quoted as saying, "Seems like every performance, the judges kept having all these crotches shoved in their faces . . . I mean, hello?"

Now the operative words here were, "I mean, hello?" That phrase really belongs to me for use in this work and I kind of resent its being usurped by my good friend. Besides which, I would be much happier if the Technical Committee would concentrate on a subject that everyone knows I have been promoting for years, and that is the subject of pointed toes (see chapter 2). Charlie Cyr, you see, can and often does show folks that he can point his toes. He does this by taking off his shoes, turning his toes under and then walking around on the front of the foot with the toes curled under and back. (Ouch!)

If the Technical Committee would only forget being negative about crotch shots and costumes and concentrate on being positive about spreading the word about Charlie's pointed toes, everyone would learn something instead of having to unlearn something yet again.

Maybe a little further explanation here would be helpful. You see, there are two rules relating to clothing: Rule #500 and Rule #612. Rule #500 is for single and pair skaters, and Rule #612 is for ice dancers.

Rule #500 says that clothing "must not give the effect of excessive nudity for athletic sport." (Does that mean excessive nudity is OK as long as it is *not* for athletic sport?) But I wonder, since everyone wants figure skating to be considered a "sport," why can't skaters wear something skimpy as competitors do in swimming, where the costuming would make a G-string look fat?

Rule #500 also says that men must wear trousers; no tights are permitted. But Rule #612 says that male ice dancers must wear "full length" trousers, and that the man's costume may not be sleeveless. It also says the ladies must wear a skirt!

OK. Let's remember that Debi Thomas wore a unitard in her Short Program at the 1988 Olympic Winter Games in Calgary. It was black with some decoration around the top. As always, she had a spectacular presence and looked sensational. So, while the rules required a skirt for ice dancing, the rules did not require a skirt for ladies in the single events.

Maybe, therefore, since the ISU also covers speed skating, the ISU could make a rule that would kill several birds with one stone. We could call it the "Debi Thomas Rule," and it would ban all speed skaters and all figure skaters (and why not all swimmers, too?) from wearing anything like a unitard or tights unless it had something around the waist like a skirt and was not sleeveless and maybe had a section of trousers that only covered the bottom of the legs and were therefore "full length"! (Can I be serious?)

And while I am at it, what about clothing rules for bobsledders, who want to cut any friction from air rushing by as they plummet down the mountain and therefore wear skin-tight uniforms that would show a feather if it had the temerity to sneak its way in?

The men's competition in the 1998 Olympic Winter Games in Nagano was a costume eye-opener. Ilia Kulik skated to George Gershwin's *Rhapsody in Blue*. He moved out in a yellow and black geometric but irregularly patterned, shiny vinyl top under a white vest with black pockets over black pants. It looked, many said, like a giraffe! It took me aback. But so had George Gershwin's composition taken aback the audience in 1924 when jazz was just being introduced.

I found it to be a costume of substance; one that made me think. I thought maybe it was referencing the splotched elements of postmodern art: semi-geometric in design with flat, blatant, solid colors. Most important, in my mind, it was not the obvious blue costume of every other *Rhapsody in Blue* performance the skating world had seen. It related to the modernity of Gershwin's time, when the impact of his masterpiece mesmerized audiences everywhere.

I suppose some designer could have assembled something that took more of an Art Deco, Art Moderne or even lyrical feel, but this leap forward was refreshingly unusual, and it got to me.

The question remains, however, was there a concept in his choice of costume that melded with choreographic interpretation of *Rhapsody in Blue*? Remember, Ilia Kulik was Russian and grew up during the powerful but controlling times of the Soviet Union when it seemed everything was attributed to being Russian. Wasn't jazz invented in Vladivostok (not New Orleans), and hadn't it come up the Volga to Moscow (and not the Mississippi)? (I apologize to my Russian friends, but it was a controlling time.)

I thought maybe Kulik was recalling the look that jazz folk adopted in Harlem in the 1920s when wild yellow suits, splashy ties, orange shoes, and broad-brimmed hats sparked up the world of entertainment. After all, it was the age of jazz and Gershwin lived at 110th Street, just blocks away from the Cotton Club. Gershwin, even in his school days (which he quit at fifteen), went to Harlem, where Black Man's Blues and his own wild New York energy got mixed together. It was skyscraper time and the city was all about people reaching for the sky to get ahead! The scales he chose were combinations of black and white keys, major and minor, rising up to the top. His energy came out in his frantically tapping the keys, contrasted with the lyrical moods of Black Blues.

The effect must have been as compelling as the psychedelic sounds of the '60s later were.

Could that have been the influence and the concept for Kulik? His performance featured some of the best upright landings (had he swallowed a gyroscope for balance?). But his skating was characterized by casual, unfocused body positions. There was no great combination of wild energy (reaching for the top of the skyscraper) with the blues of Harlem. There were several upward-swinging arm movements that suggested the lyrical upward swings of the musical phrasing. Ilia is clearly a musical skater, but the choreography showed little inventiveness, nor did it reflect the combined musical elements of Gershwin's masterpiece. The moves he employed were the same as those he'd used in earlier competitions and have remained a staple of every performance since.

I concluded that while I liked the imaginativeness of

the costume, there was little to recommend the choreography. It seemed to be missing any overall concept called for by the music. Where was the energy of the city or the lyricism of the Blues of Harlem? So I felt it deserved high marks for the music and costume and much lower marks for the choreography and concept.

After the competition, I congratulated Tatiana Tarasova, the highly talented teacher and choreographer, on her success in guiding Ilia to an Olympic gold medal. She smiled and, turning to me, said, "Thank you, but I had nothing to do with it. He does what he wants. I just held his coat."

It is said that all creative attempts (which includes those in skating) are subject to multiple reactions. They are welcome and, if successful, at least in our eyes, they make us think outside the box—something that, unfortunately, doesn't happen often enough.

As the dance world well knows, such magic did occur in 1912. Sergei Diaghilev, the wildly dramatic and inventive Russian creator of the Ballets Russes, staged a production of *Prelude to the Afternoon of a Faun* composed by Claude Debussy. Vaslav Nijnsky was both the performer and choreographer, and wore a costume designed by Leon Bakst of almost naked faun–like design.

The costume, the music, the choreography, and the set were all inspired by the paintings on ancient Greek vases where the figures are depicted in two-dimensional form effecting side-facing moves and steps. Every element of the performance was geared to heighten this effect.

How difficult and rare it is to see such totality in a skating program under the ever more restrictive rules, and the time constraints in an Olympic sport. (Repeat: *sport!*)

But even though this is a sport, imagination and total concept can be achieved, despite the fact that the Rulebook resembles a traffic manual for a veritable Niagara Falls of changes and restrictions that constantly cascade down on the competitive world of skating. And if you think that's a mixed metaphor, take a look at the rules themselves!

An example of what is possible is one that used the same Debussy piece. It was an exhibition program that Janet Lynn skated in 1971. The choreography was by Slavka Kohout. The overall concept called for the simplest of light blue gauzy costumes, while the choreography reflected the long, slow, dream-like lyricism of Debussy's music. The concept was achieved first by long, slow, deep breaths; stretching moves as if waking from an afternoon sleep; and then long, quiet edges. The slow spacing of edges and the delayed movements complemented the music. It was truly an elegant, sensitive, thoughtful, and totally conceived performance, highlighted by leans of the body and languorous but technically solid movements.

An aside: this concept was made for an exhibition program. It would be ruinous for a competitor, as too much time was used up with no jumps, spins, turns, Twizzles, kicks, hokey-pokey moves, and flailing changes of body positions, all of which garner *points* in a competitive program—even though they remind one of drunken windmills on speed! Years earlier, Jacques Favart, then President of the International Skating Union (ISU), when challenged by someone as to the minimum quantity of jumps and spins, replied, "But she skated, sir." (For the record, Jacques Favart was the last president of the ISU who was a figure skater—and that was more than forty years ago!)

That could have been said in this instance, too. Please remember this when we get to the chapter on Short and Long Programs. I hope you will then understand my theory of what "could be" for the world of the fine art of competitive skating.

In a different vein (and in yet again another "aside"), viewers should be alert to "costume mishaps" which sometimes occur. A "mishap" (unlike a "malfunction" or some other planned idiocy that might occur when one performs at the Super Bowl) are when pants split during a split jump or a zipper pulls apart, or when the sleeve of an ice dancer catches on the hook of his partner's boot and, being made of stretchable woven sweater-like material, can stretch and stretch and stretch and stretch for several yards, leaving this "expert commentator" guffawing uncontrollably on air.

We all should admire original and inventive costuming. It is one of the things that separates skating from swimming or hockey, where the clothing is limited to being "necessary."

Since the costume wildness of much of the twentieth century, there has been a major shift toward costumes that are simpler, more conservative, less garish, and considerably more elegant. Sometimes they can be fun (note the snake that designer Vera Wang had crawling around Evan Lysacek's collar when he won the gold medal at the 2010 Winter Olympics in Vancouver). They are less adventurous because the Rulebook says, "Clothing of Competitors must be modest, dignified and appropriate for athletic competition—not garish or theatrical in design. Clothing may reflect the character of the music . ."

Well, that is that, and so much for imagination, and for Pete's sake don't tell anyone that going to the theater (or being theatrical) can be like catching the flu. Is there a skater around who doesn't want to be theatrical in some form or another? Who is writing these rules?

Costumes at the 2013 World Championships in London, Ontario seemed to be following the principle that they "should arrest the eye but not assault it." When we watch the upcoming Winter Olympics, we should note the direction costumes are taking, with a lot of gray and brown and other one-color outfits. While I'm not a fan of excessive stuff on costumes, I respect the inventive imagination of a "giraffe" costume by Ilia Kulik anytime, or something that will knock my socks off.

If Johnny Weir, who has constantly thought "out of the

box" (sometimes *very* far out of the box, but then!) had made a return and skated in Sochi, then we would have seen what I suspect would have been an unusually quiet costume of elegant design. He would have saved the wild extravagance for some headdress or other tomfoolery for the Kiss and Cry, like a wreath of roses, which he once put on his head and wore with pride in the Kiss and Cry, reverting to his usual flair when the program was over. Or was it a crown of thorns? (Did I say that?)

Wanna bet? (FYI I'm a notoriously poor gambler, and Weir has already stated that he will not make a run for Sochi, and, as every skater knows, he is commentating for the sport).

4 IS THAT MUZAK TO MY EARS?

While the skater is establishing a starting position on the ice, we hear the host announcer explain who is skating, the skater's competitive record, where the skater comes from, his or her current standings, and favorite ice cream flavor. Usually the announcer is impeccable about finishing all of this before the skater begins the program.

Then we hear the music and the skater starts the program. It is the music that sets the tone and supports the concept, the costume, and the theme of the performance (let's hope!). The music is the basis for the program that we are about to see. Remember, the skater should inhabit the character or interpret the idea or the feeling behind a piece of music.

Some skaters have great musicality and skate with the music. Some skaters chase the music, always trying to catch up, like that last skater on the end of the pinwheel line in the Ice Capades who finally catches up—but only just as the pinwheel ends.

Now, if you don't mind another sideways slant on things far removed, let me tell you that when the Broadway musical *A Funny Thing Happened On the Way to the Forum* starring Zero Mostel was doing its out-of-town tryout, the producers felt the opening song was not good. They called in renowned choreographer Jerome Robbins as the "play doctor." He asked, "What is the play about?" They talked, and he kept repeating his question, "What is the play about?" Finally someone blurted out, "Well, It's about comedy!" Robbins then said, "Then go write a song about comedy!" They composed the opening song "Comedy Tonight," and that number as well as the musical itself became a smash.

My point here is that the skater should know what the music is about. What is it saying? What is its history, its emotional impact, for both the skater and for the audience? Is the skater merely skating in spite of the music and thinking about launching into the first jump (which is probably the most difficult move) and to heck with the music? If you are going to skate to the "Rose Adagio" from *The Sleeping Beauty* or to a selection from *Les Misérables*, you should understand what the music is saying.

Skaters who famously understood their music were champions like John Curry, Robin Cousins, Kurt Browning, Michelle Kwan (particularly when skating to *Scheherazade*), Dorothy Hamill, Paul Wylie, Janet Lynn, ice dancers Torvill and Dean and Blumberg and Seibert, pairs like Gordeeva and Grinkov and Shen and Shao of China, and many others who have enriched our enjoyment of the Fine Art of Figure Skating with their musical sensitivity.

Back in the dark ages (i.e., in my day), the music was primarily classical. We were not allowed to use vocal music (which is inching its way into the competitive scene today), so we chose the non-vocal parts of operas and operettas, as well as excerpts from ballet scores, symphonies, and particularly overtures. The powers that be would have run screaming from the room if anyone had dared to use a version of "That's Amore" (with a lyric like "when the moon hits your eye like a big-a pizza pie, that's amore") or some other popular song, although once in a while "How High the Moon" was used for exhibition programs. These were not considered to be "serious" enough.

I recall selections from *The Thieving Magpie*, *Rhapsody in Blue*, *Graduation Ball*, *Hungarian Rhapsodies*, *Zampa*, *The Comedians*, and *If I Were King*. They were popular because they were sedate, conventional, and proper for the traditional world of skating and because they had beginnings, middles, and ends—that is, they were more or less musically complete in themselves. They also could be edited down to fit the time requirements.

The great problem was cutting the music to the right size. The Free Skate program for the men was five minutes, with a plus or minus leeway of ten seconds. Today it is four-and-a-half minutes. That extra thirty seconds could be a killer, particularly in high-altitude places like the old Broadmoor Skating Arena in Colorado Springs, where many U.S. and World competitions were held and where many memories were made. It is now demolished.

We did not have the luxury of today's digital magic for editing our music. One had to literally cut tape and try to splice it together as best one could. Sometimes this was not successful, and screeching sounds like the scraping of fingernails on a blackboard or like the grinding of gears in a stick shift car would freeze our berries! As a result, music that could easily be cut to the time limits was used.

(Do any of you who are too young to be sitting on the couch with us remember when one had to manually shift gears on a car? Of course you don't, you dear little teenyboppers!)

Today, music is sometimes created for skaters or played live, a luxury we did not have except for exhibitions at "exotic" places like the Wembley Arena in London. There, music in my day was played by a live orchestra. There was minimal time to rehearse, and it was difficult getting the conductor to play at the speed needed.

But part of the musical fun back then was seeing the ice being resurfaced. There was no Zamboni machine. The men who swept the ice did so like a military marching band. Each one would march in a diagonal line angled slightly to the front of the other, from end to end of the rink. It all seemed choreographed as each sweeper pushed to a synchronized rhythm in unison with the audience, who clapped in time with them! I guess it was an early version of the fifth-inning ritual in baseball games at Yankee Stadium when everyone sings "YMCA" and pretends they're the Village People.

Today, skaters perform to pop, hip-hop, rhythm and blues, classical music, and film scores, and are blessed with elaborate state-of-the-art editing equipment and engineers. But even today, skaters keep returning to a handful of pieces of music.

There are many *Carmens*, Swan *Lakes*, "Nessun Dormas," and selections from *Les Misérables* and Charlie Chaplin films. Why? Because they're easy to skate to, have lyrical, sweeping melodies that support edging, and mostly because they're familiar. The skaters feel comfortable with the familiar and with music that provides a wide range of styles and some variations of rhythms.

Music that turns out to be magical for skating generally ends up used *ad nauseum*. Carmen got herself stabbed so many times I have lost track, so can't we let her die in peace? And anyone who uses *Swan Lake* should remember that it comes with more than a century of history of elegance, musical completeness, and choreography that requires body positions where the skater should have at least some classical training.

More challenging for skating are choices like Dave Brubeck's "Take Five" (a complex step rhythm difficult for skaters other than peerless ice dancers such as Torvill and Dean).

The rules, I feel, burden the skater with countless step sequences, choreographic sequences, and linking movements. As a result, much of skating today is frenetic and overloaded with windmilling arm positions, head tipping, bending at the waist, and endless filibuster moves that contribute nothing to the overall impact of the choreography. How many times do we see skaters moving down the ice and suddenly one arm will shoot up into the air for no apparent reason—unless perhaps the skater is trying to hail a cab. Programs today are so full of pecking and pointing moves that one would think someone might soon choose to skate to "Pick-A-Little, Talk-A-Little, Cheep! Cheep! Cheep!" from *The Music Man.* (Sorry! I just might have to take that back!)

Music for clogging or step dancing can be difficult. It is harder to create flow with it. Torvill and Dean and others have achieved successful programs using these rhythms, but they are not always their most impressive works.

The music that Fred Astaire and Ginger Rogers danced to was ballroom, and that worked for ice dancing. Traditionally it was used for compulsory dances like a waltz, foxtrot, tango, blues, or quickstep, all of which were precisely outlined in the Rulebook.

Music by Lady Gaga (used mostly in exhibitions) works when Johnny Weir uses it. But whatever originality there is in Beyoncé's "Put a Ring On It" or in the deadening, repetitive, non-rhythms of Cold Play could, would, and do escape me (sorry, Gwyneth Paltrow).

After all, though I hate to remind you, I am an Octogenarian Skating Professor. But while I respect the past, I also admire the present. Let us not forget that there were many creations in the past that no longer see the light of day. The world today is both sophisticated and knowledgeable about music and its history, from Bach to Beethoven to bunga bunga music, and it's invigorating to have so many choices.

The classic dilemma of how to make music conform to the skating rules played out with ice dancers Torvill and Dean's performance to Maurice Ravel's *Bolero* in the 1984 Olympic Winter Games in Sarajevo. The problem occurred over twenty-three seconds at the start. Christopher Dean and his coach, Betty Callaway, were both perfectionists and were loath to edit out essential phrasing, no matter what the rules were. They read the rules carefully and found that the rules called for the timing of the program to start when the "skating" began, but not when "movement" or the music began. So "T and D" knelt on the ice at the start, moving and swaying, but not skating. No music was mangled. The piece remained sensitively arranged and the performance became the most famous ice dance in the history of skating.

Had T and D not found a way around the rules' ridiculous stringencies, the world of skating would not have had the benefit of a perfect program.

However, the plot thimkens! (Thimkens? Yes, thimkens!) The Technical Committee got back at them and promptly negated kneeling on the ice, decreed that the time clock would start with any movement (I wonder if the clock would start if Katarina Witt checked her hair pin after she was at center ice?), and refused to permit any lying on or being thrown across the ice which, for those who remember it, was the astonishing climax of the program.

Hasn't the element of danger—of falling, slipping, and sliding on the ice—been part of the magical world of skating since the beginning of time, and why shouldn't they be part of the choreographed concept (remember Paul Wylie's long slides on one and both of his knees)? No sirree! We can't have any of that in our rarified world of high class performance.

The point is that skaters, as well as the members of the Technical Committee who create the rules, and the head honchos of the ISU who guide the Technical Committee's directions and actions and also edit their decisions, should feel and understand that there is a history, story, and reason for most of the music and the choreography that skaters elect to use. Just to listen to and relate to the rhythms is not enough. Nor is it sufficient to just demand that it be so many minutes and seconds long. We're not talking about a speed skating race, where a fraction of a second more or less may determine the outcome.

In the Torvill and Dean *Bolero* story, the history of the music is informative. The Russian ballerina Ida Rubenstein, who was born in 1885 to a wealthy family, was a provocative performer who danced with Diaghilev's Ballets Russes and also created her own ballet company. She sought out Maurice Ravel. It was well known that she asked him to create a work for her that would be of Spanish influence. One can envision him saying, as composers are apt to do, "I will go to my trunk," where pieces written earlier were stored. He had written a piece that, it was said, he used for teaching the principles of orchestration. It had little form, minimal contrast, and little melodic development, but it did have a gradual building of force and power as more and more instruments came online in the composition. (One might say that the piece reflected and mimicked the repetitive soundings of machinery which, in a certain way, was somewhat related to George Gershwin's *Rhapsody in Blue*, where the nervous tapping energy of New York was evident.) It became *Bolero*.

The ballet was an instant success when it was first produced at the Paris Opera in 1928 with choreography by Bronislava Nijinska, the sister of the great dancer Vaslav Nijinsky. The continued later success of the piece sometimes angered Ravel, as it had been written not for performance but for instruction.

Since then, *Bolero* has been choreographed by many others. The original version involves dancing in a café where a woman responds to the rising frenzy of the music, leaps on a table, and continues the wildness of the moment. At the climax of the music, which is a crashing descending explosion, she collapses, the lights go out, and the men, who have surrounded the table, start to climb onto the table. It is a sensual tour de force.

Torvill and Dean had created their own interpretation of the music, and they and their choreographer Betty Callaway were in a pickle. If they tried to cut the music too much, it would have destroyed the concept and perfection of the piece.

They also needed to figure out how to interpret the sensual sensibility of the music. (As a somewhat slanted aside, remember the creators of the figure skating rules where not always aligned with creativity.)

Torvill and Dean's persona was of the traditional English reserve. They had never joined the psychedelic world of the 1960s. The British were some of the first enthusiasts of tea dancing, ballroom dancing, and afternoons at the Brighton seashore. They also were the major forces in ice dancing from the very beginning.

Yet Torvill and Dean were also very much of today as well as of the future, and are two of the most creative forces in the world of ice dancing.

The sensuality of their *Bolero* program was achieved by the repetition and rising intensity of their movements, which paralleled the repetition and crescendo of the melody and the orchestration. But the climax was achieved by Dean's grabbing Torvill by the shoulders and twisting and torquing her body, finally throwing her on the ice and falling almost on top of her. Their almost stoic expressions and calm demeanor far removed this from pole dancing. This was an intellectual experience. Their persona never reduced it to vulgarity. But they nevertheless opened a window on what Bo Derek asked in the movie *10*: "Have you ever done it to music?"

In another of my delicious asides, I will point out that many others have attempted *Bolero*, but not always with great success. At one point I heard that Michelle Kwan had asked Christopher Dean to choreograph a piece for her to *Bolero*. I was intrigued as to what it would be and commented on my interest in it to Dean. He was adamant that I not attribute any contribution by him to its creation.

Then I saw the performance. It was an interesting introduction to the changes we all go through, the way we develop, and who we are!

Michelle had been brilliant in performing the role of Scheherazade in Nicolai Rimsky-Korsakov's composition of the same name. But Scheherazade is the role of a storyteller who must maintain the attention of the listener. Unless she keeps the sultan captivated until dawn, she will die. So Scheherazade never finished by dawn any of the stories she told, needing the next night to finish each one. When the 1001 stories were over, he had fallen in love with her and allowed her to live. (Nice going, Scheherazade!)

To perform the role of Scheherazade successfully, charm, exuberance, sweet seductiveness, intelligence, and mystery are the operative words. Michelle at twenty-two was comfortable with the tenderness of the music and the concept of the storytelling in *Scheherazade*. She was then and is today an accessible but private person. *Bolero* is a story of passion and sensuality amid the incessant pounding of the rhythm. In my opinion, *Bolero* was not her cup of tea.

Bolero is in the same genre as the classic Danse Apache. This classic dance is set in French bistros where, traditionally, the man threw the lady across the floor, took her on airplane spins, flipped her over his head, and swirled her on the floor. All moves that are old-time favorites in the world of ice shows but that are disallowed in competition!

So, ice dancers, forget the Danse Apache unless you can figure out a way to subvert the rules.

Like T and D did.

And while I'm at it, let's not forget that dances like *The Dying Swan, Romeo and Juliet,* and so many more may be off the plate if you want to be free to tell the story realistically. No sirree! Don't even think of it.

The huge variety of music from which to choose, coupled with the advanced editing technology available today, offers truly exciting options for skating program music. Back in the dark ages when I started out, we brought our music to competitions in the form of 78 records. They were breakable, easily scratched, or marred by dropped needles, which had to be set carefully onto the record. One had to bring extra copies, carry them separately, and protect them with your life, otherwise you would be skating to the national anthem of whatever country you were in.

I was pleased when it became acceptable to use a much wider variety of music, including movie sound tracks: Paul Wylie's programs to *JFK* and *The Untouchables* and *Schindler's List*, and Todd Eldredge's performance to *1492* were exhilarating. The music provided superb bases for dramatic concepts and choreography.

But even with all the options available, skaters still make musical missteps. Consider the deadening stuff some of us call "music by the yard," or "taxi cab music," or "elevator music."

Skaters need music that will create magic. With the right choice, the music will lead the skater to create a "painting" (and lead us to see it). It can tell a story, set a mood, provide highs and lows, and places for starts and stops. It can also provide "negative space"—which can be silence, or a change in dynamics that allows the skater to frame an element, a move, a separate choreographic sequence, or an idea (if we can keep meaningless arm flailings from ruining the moment in the constant struggle to wring out another point!). It should provide a beginning, a middle, and an end. It should inspire a concept that will bring us to our feet. It can and should demand and get the very best out of the skater.

So, skaters of the world, unite! And choose your music carefully. It should lift and inspire you to do your best.

And while I am at it, remember rules are meant to be broken—thank you, T and D!

5 "OPEN YOUR EYES, DUMMY!"

Sometimes it takes a little something extra to get us to "open our eyes." And in skating, like just about anything else in life, it is critical to open your eyes and your mind so you understand what the task is and how to meet your goal, whether it's learning to do a Shoot the Duck as a very young skater, or going for the gold at the Olympics.

The art of teaching, as well as the art of learning, is a sublime gift. Not every teacher nor every student has it. But those who do have a gift from God. Teaching and learning are constant processes. In skating, it is not necessary that a teacher be a champion. But it is also not sufficient for someone to simply join the Ice Skating Institute (ISI) or United States Figure Skating (USFS) or the Professional Skaters Association (PSA) (all of which are worthy organizations). What is necessary is to continue learning from everything and not let the constipated rules of competition that are in play today limit "seeing" and pose a barrier to being creative.

Reviews of videos, understanding music, and seeing great choreography and outstanding performances both in and out of the field of skating are essential for defining and refining one's taste and expanding one's capacity to create.

As a convoluted aside, but one with a purpose, let me tell you that when I was six and suffering from a burst of "zealous parents" wanting their children "to have everything," my brothers and I were given swimming lessons, tennis lessons, riding lessons, piano lessons, shooting lessons at the local Gun Club, and even a class in tap dancing.

There is a film of me at age six or so with a friend from kindergarten doing a soft shoe dance on the lawn to the tune of "Tea for Two." A large black pet dog was sitting on the grass between us, and every time we soft-shoed near the dog, I could be seen patting it on the head in time with the music and the steps. Fred Astaire, here we come!

No, I will not show you this film. It is not on YouTube or anyplace else because I know you will criticize the fact that I didn't try to do something I couldn't, like a Biellmann pull-up while simultaneously patting the dog (now, *that* would get points!), and also that the dog's feet aren't pointed.

I do not remember the teacher who taught us this "Tea for Two" extravaganza, but I do know that the music, the movement, my friend, and the dog all made it an enjoyable experience. Enjoyment is one of the most important aspects of both teaching and learning.

Later, my mother took me skating at a rink in Riverdale, New Jersey. I learned in no time to do a sit spin, or at least something that passed in my mind as a sit spin. I would do it every time someone came through the door. I guess it was an early onset of being a show-off. (No retorts here, please!)

When I was eleven, my ever-frugal mother bought me a present of "10 Lessons for the Price of 9." This led me to taking my first figure skating test. (There were eight tests, the last being the Gold Test). These were all tests of skating figures, starting with a simple figure eight where you skated one circle on the right foot and one on the left, making a figure eight! Then there were more and more elaborate figures, including "one-foot" eights, three-lobed figures, and figures that included "three turns," "brackets," "counters," "rockers," "double threes," "loops," "change loops," and "loop change loops." It took years to learn all 41 figures, each of which were precisely set out in the Rulebook. In skating there is always a rulebook. The United States Figure Skating Association (now called U.S. Figure Skating or USFS) had one that covered figures (when they were in existence), and so did the International Skating Union (ISU), which governs skating around the world. These rules today are changed as frequently as the once-famous Sears Catalogue was, and perhaps should be used for the same purpose. (If you don't get it, forget it!)

Don't ask me to describe all of these figures, because the Fine Art of Figure Skating doesn't include figures in world or Olympic competitions anymore. While the eight tests are still in existence, they are seldom given because the number of judges capable and knowledgeable enough is diminishing rapidly. Substitutions like "moves in the field" have replaced the entire story and value of learning to skate figures. So we will not be seeing real figures while slouching on this couch unless the television network needs to fill time with historical segments—which sometimes becomes necessary when the Games are held in different time zones halfway around the world.

The figures were, many thought, too dull, too boring, took too much time, had too little excitement, were too costly, and had no income potential for television.
A death knell if ever there was one.

When I took my first figure test, I failed miserably. "Don't skate so near the hockey barrier, little boy." "Oh," I said, "I know what I'm doing,"—and promptly skated into the barrier.

Then the time came for the Annual Skating Carnival, an exhibition with music, costumes, some homemade sets, and a few simple production numbers. I thought I might have an opportunity to skate something called a "solo" and display my sit spin. Others did not think so. I was assigned the role of a grasshopper. But I remained enthusiastic.

Sensing this, my father asked the teacher if I should have more lessons. I was then five feet tall, weighed 160 pounds, and looked like a butterball. Taking one look, the teacher said I would never learn to skate 'til a "snowball learned to live in Hades."

The luck of the draw was that I never heard this, and that the one person who should have heard it—my father—did. It was the best impetus for my getting the best training available. My father could be like a bull with steam coming out of his ears if someone said something was not possible for his family.

So my father arranged for me to take lessons in New York City at a rink that was, at that time, installed in Roseland (later a dance hall), in the West 50s. The teacher was a dapper, very short, English ice dancer named Joe Carroll. He was a ladies man through and through; wore spats, a vest, and kid gloves, and taught the ladies how to dance on ice while simultaneously dazzling them.

He advised my father that if we were serious, we should go to Lake Placid in upstate New York in the Adirondack Mountains where the 1932 Olympic Winter Games were held. We went.

There I met Gustave Lussi and took my first lesson from him on my thirteenth birthday.

Everything I know about the technique of skating I learned from him, and under his tutelage I won every title there was for me to win for a period of ten years (every title, that is, except for two, but all of which were incredible learning experiences.)

I describe all this because good teaching can be the crux of good learning . . . as long as the pupil has an open and receptive mind and a desire to learn.

The lucky thing for me was that Gustave François Lussi, who had been a ski jumper, was a teacher who not only taught by precise examples of every position but who also intrigued us with his enthusiastic embrace of many other skating elements, as well as other subjects. He was an inspiring teacher.

Lussi was Swiss, and almost as much of a precision operation as a Swiss watch. He was married to one Thelma MacDowell, a lady of great beauty and an occasional ice dancer. Her face was framed with long braids. She skated in the most elegant lilting style highlighted by graceful, pointed feet. She wore edelweiss designs on her clothes and in her hair the edelweiss flowers her husband grew.

I never called them by their first names. Eventually, years later, I started calling them the "Duke and Duchess" to signify both familiarity and respect.

His family tree, beginning in 1307, was stenciled on the wall of the Town Hall of Stans, Switzerland following an act of bravery by an early Lussi in a long-forgotten local battle. He was never lax in either clothing or manner and always reflected the controlled, precise persona of a true Swiss. He was always dressed in a jacket, shirt, and tie, and his trousers were seamed down their length so they didn't lose their crease in the moisture of the rink. He wore blue suede skates as long as he could, and then stood at the rink edge. He never, ever leaned over the barrier or on it, never screamed instructions at his pupils, and never insulted them. Every request to do a move or to repeat something was followed by "please." It was a gentleman's approach to teaching and nothing at all like the manner of too many younger teachers today whose pupils are often reduced to tears from a teacher's insults. In addition, too many teachers today can do moves, but can't teach them: "This is the way it's done, so watch me."

A good teacher, I feel, is one who lets pupils make the learning experience their own. Pupils should not be simply parrots repeating something back. Movement needs to be internalized by the skater and then produced from the inside out. Gustave Lussi taught each skater to do each move, and never by parroting him. Yet he also knew how to do the basic moves of skating superbly.

So, dear friends on the couch (and you other skaters who are supposedly pretty hot skaters), let me challenge you. Can you do a "clean" three turn? I have to assume you know that if you turn a figure skate upside down, the blade, which is about three-eighths of an inch wide, has two edges running the length of the blade. One is the inside edge; the other is the outside edge, and you can lay a pencil in the valley between the two edges. Gustave Lussi could skate a perfect forward three turn. To visualize what this is, grab a pen and one of those napkins on the coffee table. Now draw the number 3 and then connect the ends to make a full circle. When doing a three turn, the skater changes from the forward outside edge to the back inside edge precisely at the center of the three, leaving an open space the width of the blade. The change of the edge should not occur before the exact tip of the three, nor after.

Now for anyone on this couch who is a skater, please try it on clean ice, look down carefully, and examine the ice closely to see if you can do a perfect three turn with that very small open space correctly placed. Do not for one moment think it is easy.

At the edge of every piece of ice Gustave Lussi taught on was a blackboard. Each position in a spin or figure or jump was drawn in chalk, described precisely or shown clearly. We were never without a clear example of what our position should be. It was this that kept us almost always securely positioned. He drew stick figures to show us the body positions. In a sit spin, the body should be shaped like a tilted "Z". Note Dorothy Hamill's perfect position in a sit spin and you will see what I mean. Her back is straight as an arrow as she leans forward in the sitting position. Her arms are stretched and not allowed to rest sloppily on her knees, and the leg from the hips to the knee is parallel to the ice. This is the basic sit spin position. It is not the same as a "cannonball" sit spin, where the back is intentionally rounded.

So there! to the naysayers who can't see what each position should and could be and who let their fanny sink toward the ice in a sit spin and collapse the back—rather than watching and working to get it to be an elegant move as Dorothy Hamill did.

I often think that Gustave Lussi's precise positioning of all parts of the body was what was responsible for the minimal injuries his pupils suffered. Admittedly we weren't trying to do quads from age eleven on. But even so, it seemed that the stress and strain on the body were minimal. I attribute that to proper positioning. What I did feel was utter confidence in his teaching.

Many times I have heard youngsters who've had a few lessons and think they know everything complain that a new teacher wasn't teaching a particular move properly. I've always felt that the first thing a student should do is learn it the way the teacher says; then, after you can do it their way, make up your own mind as to the best method. (But then, what do I know?)

Now, let me beg your patience and do a really bad waltz jump into another era. When I was twenty-two and in law school, after I had won two Olympic gold medals and retired from competition, I took up dance seriously (as seriously, that is, as one can while going to law school and simultaneously skating in the Ice Capades). I studied with every well-known dance teacher I could. Among them were Igor Youskevich, Leon Danielian, Alexandra Danilova, Luigi, and Nanette Charisse. The problem was, I wasn't "getting it."

I always stayed in the back of the class. I felt I could do better *jetés*, *pirouettes* and *tours en l'air* to the left than half the class. But they looked like dancers and I didn't.

In dance, turning "to the left" means turning counter-clockwise; turning "to the right" would be clockwise. While dancers do turns and moves in both directions to accommodate choreography, skaters usually turn in same direction for both their jumps and spins. Each skater usually has one direction that is easier for turning, and each skater turns in his or her "natural direction."

To find out your natural direction, put down your beer, stand up, and then jump in the air and try to do a partial or full turn. (If you are my age, forget the jump and just do a simple turn on the floor!) You will automatically turn to either the right or left and that is your "natural" direction. The reason skaters concentrate on one direction is because they have to rotate exceedingly fast in both jumps and spins. Turning in one direction for jumps and spins helps to educate the body's "muscle memory" for doing fast turns. This helps skaters achieve the greatest number of rotations possible in a jump. In order to be more versatile, some skaters do simpler jumps and spins in both directions for choreographic interest.

So, one day, I took a class with Nanette Charisse, the sister-in-law of famed dancer Cyd Charisse. Remember her siren number with Gene Kelly in the MGM movie *Singin' in the Rain?* I waited until the end of the class, after the others had left, and then stomped over to Nanette with smoke coming out of my ears. I was livid. When she asked what she could do for me, I angrily responded, "I'll tell you what you can do for me! I can do better *tours, jetés,* and *pirouettes* to the left than half the dancers in the class, but they look like dancers and I look like a clumsy skater! What's the problem?"

She thought for a moment, looked at me seething, and then calmly (how I dislike someone else's ability to stay calm in what I considered to be a *major* crisis!) and asked, "Well, what do they look like?"

In total fury, I marched back to the center of the studio, saying, "I'll show you!" I then proceeded to pull up my core body position, keep my shoulders lowered, my stomach in, my chin in, my head high, and my spine and neck stretched and pulled up, and proceeded to do a *tour en l'air* (a jump of one or multiple turns in the air from a standing position).

I wasn't used to this type of positioning and nearly fell on my face. But Nanette said, "There, now you look like a dancer!" My jaw dropped. All this time I had been practicing at the barre (the dance barre, not the drinks bar!) and had been taught to hold my core position properly, but never had it actually "registered." As I mentioned in the Introduction, skating may be all in the eye of the beholder, but it is also in whether the brain registers what the eye beholds. I cannot tell you how many times I have seen young folk (like I did) take a dance class, learning proper core positions, and then when they move onto the ice, simply revert to their old, more relaxed (read casual) positions.

This may sound simplistic, but Nanette Charisse's method at that moment got me to register and apply what I had been taught for so long. (Which reminds me of the old saying that the teacher can teach best when the student is ready to learn).

An additional gift of this insight was that when you tuck in your tummy and stretch and pull your spine up through the back of your head, it also affects your extremities. You are not likely to leave your legs hanging like sausages in the window at Shultze's Meat Market, nor will your arms be left hanging sloppily without your knowing that they are in lazy and incomplete positions. It doesn't work to try to stretch your legs and point your feet without starting from the center of the core.

One way to test your posture is to first put down your scotch and soda (I mean, your Diet Coke) and get up from the comfortable sofa you are sitting on.

On that sofa, your back is probably rounded to a fare-thee-well, particularly if you are totally slumped into the cushions. Sit instead on a straight-backed chair with no cushion and push your fanny all the way to the back of the chair. Suck your tummy in. You will feel your spine stretch up. Pull your spine up through your head, keep your chin in, your shoulders lowered, and your neck stretched and pulled up, too. Now you are on your way to a correct position of your core.

All this stretching is too much! Pardon me while I go lie down.

Also remember that it is possible (though it doesn't often happen) that a skater will be so straight and so pulled up that the skater's center of gravity is no longer forward over the hips. Could this be causing the sometimes wide-swinging free leg we see on too many landings? A skater who has impeccable posture might be susceptible to this. Remember that to do a good jump, one has to jump forward as well as upward.

(An aside is that both dancers and skaters need to loosen their stance a little to get into an attack position. So a short, minimal pumping (recoil?) of the body stance might be good for snapping a jump forward as well as upward.)

One can feel the principle of over-arching by other means, too. Kimmie Meissner, a recent U.S. champion and a lovely skater, has long, elegant arms. But she was over-extending them. This meant that the insides of the elbows were thrust forward and the arms were bent backwards. I suggested she hold a huge oversized beach ball in her arms. If it was large enough, she would have to keep her arms wide apart and slightly curved in order to hold the ball up. It would be too difficult to hold the ball if her elbows were over-extended. The resulting rounded arms then became like a giant open hug, which turned them into graceful positions. How many times today do we see skaters fling their arms up, over-extending them, particularly at the end of the program? She was blessed with arms that were long and elegant, and not to make the most of them would have been a loss.

Any one of us who is moving inexorably toward maturity should consider pulling up our core so that we, too, stand straight and not look like we have eaten too many potato chips or resemble an apple on toothpicks.

Body position is at the center of good skating. It is needed for jumps, spins, edging, spirals, and all the individual moves that are endlessly required to gain points in order to medal. Once one learns to stretch and pull up the core of the body, it will help give defining shape as well as strength and good alignment to the arms, head, and legs, as well as improving the take-offs, landings and all the bits and pieces of one's performance. This does not mean you need to look like classical ballet dancer. But check out the posture and positions of dancers and skaters like Gene Kelly, Fred Astaire, Kurt Browning, Scott Hamilton, and assorted others, and you will see proper body placement that is not overdone but well placed.

In 1961, I produced for CBS Sports a Memorial Show at the Boston Arena for the victims of the plane crash in Belgium that took the lives of the entire U.S. World Figure Skating team. All of us got together to honor their memory. It was the last skating exhibition I was to do. The music was from *Don Quixote*. I am more pleased with this performance than with other more technically difficult programs I had done. I felt that finally I understood what position, what stretch, and what focus our body should have. As I have said too many times to count: "Too soon oldt, too late schmart! Small satisfactions for small folks.

But it's in these small but hard-won satisfactions that the true joy in teaching, learning, and skating resides.

6 CENTERING

How many times has the kid in all of us tried to spin a top and keep it from careening off the table? A skating spin should be like a spinning top, turning steadily and evenly in one spot, without wobbling or lurching in ever-larger circles or "traveling" toward the edge of the table (or barriers of the skating rink).

The most important thing is that a spin be "centered" and not travel. Yet all too often we see the TV camera keeping the skater spinning in one spot in the middle of the screen (the camera crew is superb at keeping the focus on the skater)—while the audience behind them appears to be moving sideways! Keep your eye out for this, and when you see the advertisements on hockey barriers moving either to the right or the left during a skater's spin, look closer and check it out. The spin is not centered when this happens. The skater is traveling and not spinning in one spot. A spin should always be judged on its centering as well as on its speed, steadiness, and the skater's position(s).

Some spins are *intended* to be slow and even languorous. Other spins can look like a top spinning so fast it might get a speeding ticket. At one time these blurred spins were called "killer" spins. In any spin it is the

67

centering that is critical, and in a fast spin it is even more what controls and keeps the spin on a steady level.

Anyone sitting on the couch watching should be aware of the new International Judging System (IJS), which was instituted following the 2002 Salt Lake Olympics pair skating scandal and which affects the judging of spins. Look for changes of edges during the spin . . . forward edge to back edge or outside edge to inside edge (or both) Also look for the endless changes of position: camel to sit, jump-overs, broken leg positions, cross-foots, catchfoots with the free leg in front, catchfoots with the free leg in the back (a.k.a, a Biellmann spin!) and spins to the side as well as backspins and layback spins and half spins and bent spins! Each position accrues points, and don't try to count them on your fingers.

The Technical Committee has been busy as a bee!

The new rules do not sufficiently reward long, blurred or "killer" spins. But good spin ability has other benefits. Gustave Lussi taught me that spinning was the basis also for multiple revolutions in jumping. Learned properly, it helps skaters execute fast rotation in the air (for triple and quadruple rotations!). He particularly emphasized the back spin, which was the desired spinning position in most jumps.

Lussi always taught his pupils try to "blur" the forward, upright scratch spin— which, by the way, is the hardest and most difficult spin to do perfectly. In a forward scratch spin, the skater swings the free leg wide, around and in front of the skating (standing) leg. Then the skater presses the free leg across and down over the skating leg to a locked position so the free foot is over the instep of the skating foot, simultaneously pulling the arms together and then into the chest (the core of the body); and then pushing them down toward the feet, still keeping them close to the body. The object is that the legs, feet, and arms all end up held together as tightly as possible. When correctly done and truly fast, the tiniest of blood vessels would break out on the backs of the hands from the force of pulling in.

A scratch spin, as I mentioned, is a forward spin. A forward spin is one in which the skater steps onto a forward outside edge, does a three turn, and continues on a back inside edge.

An aside, please: the forward spin is more difficult to center and harder to control, but a fast, blurred, killer spin may not be worth anything more in points. Besides, a back spin is easier.

Welcome to the death knell for true, blurred, "killer" spins and spinning like a top!

So I urge all readers as well as old Pooh-Bahs like me to remember some of the great spinners, like Ronnie Robertson, Nicole Hasler, and Lucinda Ruh, or the way Dorothy Hamill does a great forward scratch spin today.

(Another aside: the reason you hear it called a "scratch" spin is because when the spin gets going really fast, the skate blade can ride up to the bottom of the toe picks instead of remaining flat on the ice, and a slight scratching sound can be heard.)

One might say that the catchfoot spin, which Denise Biellmann popularized (don't be surprised that it is therefore called a "Biellmann"), was an interesting invention. It was certainly dazzling when, during a spin, she pulled the skate of her free foot up behind her back and completely over her head. It sometimes hurt just watching it.

Today too many kids struggle to do a Biellmann. It is common to see a very young skater just starting out try to pull their leg over their head and do a Biellmann. Yet you can see they don't know how to get from point A to B in the rink. They have no clue how to skate long, sweeping edges or what a lean of the body means. Pulling the foot over the head in a Biellmann position was the sole goal. Catchfoots became so ordinary, so poorly done, and so ubiquitous that they were limited by the Technical

Committee. (There they go again. But this time their distaste was necessarily placed.)

The front catchfoot is another story. In this spin the skater raises the free leg up in front. The object is to raise the leg as high and as straight as possible. The skater holds onto the leg and pulls it into the body, which increases the rotation speed. When Alissa Czisny does it, it can be exquisite.

Skaters must not leave either the skating leg or the free leg bent in a forward catchfoot! Also, they must point the raised foot and not leave the foot almost sticking into the skater's mouth (ugh!)! As the spin gets fast, they should not allow their shoulders to sink into a rounded position and then appear to grimace in pain, which can be uglier than sin. Please, any skaters who may be on the couch with us, don't tell me the foot in a catchfoot can't be pointed and the leg can't be stretched rather than bent. If Czisny and Rudy Galindo and others can do it, so can everyone if they try!

Like learning a great spiral or a split jump, the skater needs to stretch endlessly to achieve this position in a front catchfoot. It ain't easy. Even the always-elegant Sasha Cohen can sometimes miss on this one. Note the final spin done by fifteen-year-old Russian skater Julia Lipnitskaia, where her stretch is extraordinary and the upright split extension is superb, but her back is rounded as she pulls her leg in, and the free foot is flexed (flat). That makes it "almost" a great spin. Probably few will acknowledge or understand what I am talking about.

Before you stomp off in disgust (not because of unpointed feet but because the beer is warm), let me assault you with still another aside. I should remind all and sundry that dancers "spot" the turns in their *pirouettes* (spins).

That means that they "stop" and "focus" during their turns—but for only a split second. The stop occurs with each revolution, generally when the dancer is facing the audience. You can see it when their face seems to stop moving for a split second during the turn. Spotting helps to stabilize the body and can help the dancer to finish facing the audience, which, in a theater, is usually on one side and to the front only.

Skaters don't spot because they spin much faster (thanks to less friction between skates and ice compared to feet on floor). Skaters allow their eyes to blur and not focus on any part of the background.

For those of us on the couch who aren't familiar with spins or spotting, remember that when you waltz with someone, focus on your partner's eyes. They will think you like them a lot! And it will keep you from getting dizzy.

If you allow your eyes to see different parts of the room as you turn, you may throw up into someone's décolletage! That is a no-no and certainly not the way to get a second dance or even a second chance!

As mentioned, one of the reasons we don't often see blurred or killer spins these days is that the rules don't give sufficient credit for the difficulty of a long, blurred, centered spin. Also, it can be one of the most exhausting moves, and it takes more time to execute than a quadruple combination. An Olympic skater can only do a maximum of three spins during a program, and the options that will garner the most points are relatively limited.

So why not take advantage of an easier spin or spin variation and save time and energy for other Olympian point-getting moves?

Please! Don't try to learn the rule variations, because you will find yourself getting dizzy without even turning! That can be *very* disconcerting, particularly after two beers.

Just for fun, watch the entrance to the spin. Remember, the spin needs to go from a forward motion to circular motion, which will stop it from "traveling." Look particularly at a forward camel spin (in a camel spin, the skater steps into a position on one leg where the upper body and the free leg, let's hope, will be more than parallel to the ice). This is an "arabesque" position—sort of like a one-legged swan dive.

In a "forward" camel spin (meaning entered from a forward outside edge), the skater must arrest the forward motion and turn it into circular motion. I challenge all of us on the couch to see if the skater tries and is able to rise on the toe pick when making the three turn, remain on the pick for one full turn, and then come down on the flat of the blade, still spinning. This is called "hooking" the camel. It will (the skater hopes!) stop the forward motion and center the spin.

The camel spin can sometimes be entered with too much speed. Many times you will see skaters slip off that "hook" or toe pick on the entrance and then have to quickly dip their skating knee to arrest the forward motion and center the spin. It probably will not result in any point deductions because some won't notice and others won't know what the devil I'm talking about.

There was in my day a group called the Camel Club. Members were those of us who missed the hook and ended up flat on our stomachs. This invariably included hitting your chin on the ice and splitting it open. A trip to the doctor stitched it up, everyone laughed, and you were then enrolled in the Camel Club. (I still have the scar.)

Got all that about the camel? If you didn't, don't worry! Just don't try it after a glass of wine.

One more thing. There's a variation where the skater enters the camel spin with a jump over. That's a flying camel—which was originally called a "Button Camel" (after guess who?). The "who" was fooling around one day doing camel spins. He got too close to the edge of a roped-off area where camel spins were done so that you didn't slice up another skater with the blade of your skate when you were on one leg in an arabesque position.

In order to avoid getting his legs twisted in the rope, "guess who" jumped over it. And that's how the Button Camel was invented. A serendipitous happening.

Serendipity is what British aristocrat and writer Horace Walpole called "the art of finding the unusual or the pleasantly unexpected by chance or sagacity." The name was changed from a Button Camel to a flying camel because the commentator (again, guess who?) thought it was pretentious to call a move after himself on TV.

I am now too old and too crotchety to give a rusty hoot whether someone may think something is immodest.

Have another glass of wine, Dick! (But don't have a third glass, which would lead to the "Dick Button Drinking Game"—and *that* we can do without!)

One final aside! Why was it called a camel spin in the first place? Gustave Lussi always said it was because an Australian lady named Campbell did it first and the name morphed into camel . . . whether that is true or not, I'll never know.

Then I heard it was called a camel spin because too many skaters did not stretch and arch their back and leg, allowing their fanny to stick up like the hump on a camel's back.

Then Benjamin Wright, the noted historian of figure skating, told me it was first done in the 1930s by Cecilia Colledge, the English World Champion, and was called a "parallel spin." I think maybe Charlotte Oelschlagel (who, like Madonna, went by her first name) might have done it, too, but who knows?

However the camel spin happened to get its name, it led Roone Arledge, the television sports and news producer and powerhouse behind ABC's *Wide World of Sports*, to smile wickedly and ask, "Did you ever know a camel that could fly?" And then, sometimes, ask, "Why would a camel want to fly, anyway?"

Wow! We've been talking spins for pages—and really only scratched the surface (so to speak!) of the technical difficulty of a really good blurred spin. If anyone wants to do further research, check out the rules, from Rule #8,002 all the way to Rule #12,341. (I'm joking. But maybe not!)

7 IS THERE A JUMP IN THAT JUMP?

All of us watching have to remember that jumps are the most significant element of every free skating program . . . unfortunately! Jumps should be important and in years past always were. But they were balanced by a greater emphasis on the marks given for artistic impression— which has morphed into something called Component Scores, which we'll discuss later—and by marks in the Compulsory Figures (literally varieties of figure-eights that skaters had to "draw" in the ice with their blades—a rigorous test of skill and control)—which were eliminated in one of the seismic changes in figure skating. Today, jumping is even more prominent in figure skating.

Some of the things to look for in jumping are the height and length of a jump, the smoothness and cleanness of the take-off and landing, the body positions, the speed, and the overall excitement (if any!) in the jump. Remember, too, that skaters landing a perfect jump should have as much speed coming out of the jump as they had going into it. There are other points, but let's not confuse ourselves with too much information.

A friend of mine, a sports-minded doctor whose daughter skates, turned to me in exasperation one day and said that he simply could not tell the difference between one jump and another. "How can I tell the difference?" he asked.

So, for all of us folks on the couch who are exasperated, and for all the others who are, too, but who cannot fit on the couch, let me try to give some basics about the major jumps and what we might (and might not) see at Olympic and other skating events.

Point #1: The Axel is the only jump that takes off going forward.

- All other jumps take off going backward.
- To me, the Axel is the "King of the Jumps"
- The Axel is named after Axel Paulsen, a Norwegian speed and figure skater who was born in 1855.
- The Axel takes off going forward from an outside edge on one foot and completes one-and-a-half revolutions, landing on a back outside edge on the other foot.

As an aside, I have rare 1920s film given to me by Theresa ("Tee") Weld Blanchard, who was both a single and pair skater with Nathaniel Niles. They were skating on a pond at the country club in Brookline, Massachusetts, a suburb of Boston. She is doing a dashing Axel with a landing where her back is so low it's almost touching the ice, and she was almost at a stop on the takeoff and the landing, yet it was daring and advanced for the time.

Perhaps an unnecessary aside but one that is important to me: the pair skating she displayed in that footage with Nat Niles was elegant and mesmerizing, with superior edging and flow (forgive me, but that's a "what for" to all those whippersnappers who think another catchfoot pulled over the head or a triple Salchow is all that is needed).

Point #2: All jumps are either an edge jump or a toe jump.

- Edge jumps take off from the full blade.
- Toe jumps take off from the full blade but also use the free leg and the toe picks on the free foot blade like a "pole-vault" to help lift the skater up in the air.

Point #3: The ultimate difference between one jump and another is what edge it takes off from.

- It can be from either the right or the left foot.
- It can be from an outside or an inside edge.
- It can be with or without a toe pick vault.

(Important aside: You're on an outside edge when you stand on your left foot and lean to the left. You're on an inside edge when you stand on the left foot and lean to the right. The same goes for the right foot.)

Point #4: An edge jump may be called:

- a loop
- a Salchow
- an Axel

Point #5: A toe jump may be called:

- a toe loop (a loop with a toe pick vault)
- a flip jump (a straight line entrance with a toe pick vault)
- a Lutz (takeoff from a back outside edge from the other foot from the one in a loop, and with a toe pick vault)

Pop quiz! Remember what I said above about the natural turning side? A skater usually turns easiest either to the right or left. Both ways are acceptable, like being right-handed or left-handed. Your natural turning direction is the direction you'd turn in innately if you were to jump up from a standing position and turn in the air.

If you wish to visualize these jumps, think of a devil's pitchfork, which has a handle and three prongs. The handle represents the entrance to the jump. One prong curves outward to the right. The middle prong is straight, and the third prong curves to the left. The prong that curves to the right represents the loop (toe loop). The prong in the middle represents the flip (or Salchow). The prong that curves to the left represents the Lutz. (That is, if you're a left turner. If you're a right turner, it all reverses. Devilish, eh?) There are some other jumps and hippity hops, too, but most of what you hear from the commentators will be the jumps listed above, which can be either single, double, triple, or quadruple, and can be done in combination with other jumps. Thus there's the triple Axel-triple toe loop (if the skater is very good). Or the quadruple toe loop-triple toe loop-triple toe loop. Wow!

But the really important thing (for those of us on the couch, anyway) is not to learn the different names of the jumps, but to see what *the quality* of the jump is! A perfect jump lifts up first; then the skater rotates for however many revolutions; and then a really good the skater will pause for a very short hang time and then land (you've played basketball, haven't you?). Also, a good jump should not only have height, but distance as well.

So, first of all, ask, "Is there a jump in that jump?" Meaning how high and how long is it? Secondly, the jump should impact the audience. It should inspire a small burst of exhilaration in us. It's airborne, for Pete's sake, and if it really flies, it should and would leave us breathless.

I hope you can hang in there with me for a small "Tech Talk." All of us on the couch can learn about height and distance without putting our skates on but by putting our (soft?) drinks down and moving over to stand at the bottom of the staircase. Be careful not to trip over my other dog, Carlotta, (named after Carlotta Grisi, also a 19th Century dancer) who likes to lie on peoples' feet.

Jump up onto the first step as if running up the stairs.

Now imagine you're running toward a puddle and you have to jump over it. (Let's go easy; this is not the Olympics!)

If you succeed and don't land on your face or the dog

doesn't nip at your heels, try to jump to the second step of the stairs. That's harder! Remember, you must use your arms to help lift you. The trick is to jump both *up* and *out.*

That's what the skater must do to get both height *and* distance in order to have the time to make multiple revolutions or just to soar.

OK, everyone back to the couch. We need a refill! Jumping ain't easy!

Before you try any of this on the ice, you *must* be aware that a forward edge Axel jump is the most dangerous and deadly jump of all. While the body is going forward, the skating foot can suddenly decide to make a detour to the left while the free leg goes to the right, and both your legs fly up and you fall flat as a pancake on your back.

Our bodies are built to curl inward toward our stomach, not backward. That is why we go down a ladder facing the ladder with our back to the room. So if we fall while doing a forward edge jump, it can be dangerous! When we fall from a back jump the body curls in and we most likely land on one or more soft cushions (that's short for one or more parts of our fanny).

Also look for *ballon*! *Ballon* is that effervescent nanosecond of movement that you see when a dancer jumps and at the peak of the jump there is a sudden and very slight added suspension, a split second of delay. One sees it in a tennis ball when it shivers at the peak of the bounce for the minutest bit.

Ballon is an appearance as well as the feeling of weightlessness. It's French for hang time. Skaters attempt to achieve the extra effect of *ballon* in a variation called a "delayed Axel." It was originally taught by Gustave Lussi, who had learned the principle of delay and suspension as a ski jumper.

Delayed Axels were seen more frequently during the time when single Axels where still of value. In actuality, the delayed Axel is extremely difficult, requires a greater level of control, and should be more highly valued as a worthwhile substitute for the deadening similarity of jumps currently revered by the Technical Committee.

Finally, remember that the best skaters are "jumpers" rather than merely "spinners in the air."

Since jumps are the name of the game when it comes to point-getting, it's good to know the differences in difficulty because each one gets a rating according to a set list of points. For example, a triple Axel has a point value of 8.5; a quadruple has a point value of 10.3; and then there are grades of execution and all sorts of other points we will talk about later. But please don't ask me what they all are. There's not enough popcorn to last through my recitation.

But the worst part is that if a skater attempts a quad jump (10.3 points) and falls after landing, the score he is likely to receive could be as much as if he'd done a triple jump (8.5). So of course, since there is little to lose, everyone tries a quad even knowing they may fall. That's why we see so many falls. So many, in fact, that it makes a fall seem to be an integral part of the program that is "required" by the rules and maybe even as necessary as having "an apple a day."

For some of us, it is the overall quality—the smooth entry, the height, the distance, the turns, any space or delay between the turns, and the landing—that remain the most valuable elements in a jump, regardless of whether it gets another fraction of a point or two.

(Just don't try to tell that to a skater who is hoping to medal and must be guided by the rules!)

8 WHAT'S A FALL (IN CASE YOU DON'T KNOW!)?

Back a ways I accepted an assignment to comment on a competition that turned out to be one of the less enjoyable times for me as a commentator. I was unhappy with the situation, with the folks around me, and with the quality of my own work. I was discouraged and needed to get it under control before it affected my own performance.

During a break, I got out my cell phone and called my friend Dennis Grimaldi, a successful theater producer, who was aware of my feelings. Before I could say a word, he started singing Jerome Kern's 1930s song "Pick Yourself Up," which famously urges us to "take a deep breath," dust off whatever part of us has hit the ground, and "start all over again."

I started laughing and hung up without saying a word, went right back, loosened up, and enjoyed commentating on those championships. In essence I chose to move on, to put my feelings aside. The thought from the song— "pick yourself up and dust yourself off"—was both wise and is the basic rule for how to manage a fall.

Every skater falls. Falls are part of skating. They have

been the subjects of humor, danger, injury, and excitement. They are part of every edge and every day in skating.

We always understood that if a fall occurred during a "run-through" (which is a full performance of a program, but in practice), you did not stop! EVER! You just "picked yourself up" as quickly as possible, dusted the snow off your pants, and kept going.

The snow was dusted off in the hope that it would not remind the judges of our mishap, so that perhaps they would have forgotten about it by the end of our program. The idea was to reduce *as much as possible* any negative visual effect caused by the fall and resulting break in the program. It also taught us how to keep our concentration after a fall and not lose focus or go blank on the choreography.

And lastly, you never wanted to quit or even admit that something was amiss. Of course, this was in my day and before the introduction of the new judging rules, which we've talked about, where a fall now has a mandatory deduction (but can still gain points).

Falls occur when skaters attempt jumps that are beyond their ability, when they stub a toe, when they skate too close to the hockey barriers, and for a bunch of other reasons that vary widely.

There are all kinds of falls.

There are some where you just trip (Sasha Cohen). There are falls where you lean too far over on your boot and lose the edge (that was me). Some are quick and easy, where you sit down and bounce right up so fast it seems nothing untoward occurred (Robin Cousins). We won't talk about the side slip fall (Scott Hamilton), the fall where the lady skates over her scarf (Peggy Fleming), or where the lady trips and falls on ice that has an inch of water on it, leaving herself visibly sopping wet and sprinkling water everywhere (Dorothy Hamill). Or the seemingly endless fall where the skater lands on their back with legs in the air, unable to straighten up or control their position or stop sliding across the ice from one end of the rink to the other, knocking down and becoming entangled in a curtain stretched across the ice (Suna Murray), or the two-knee slide (Kristi Yamaguchi), or the shrug-it-off fall (Judy Blumberg and Michael Seibert), or the "don't-talk-to-me-I-will-never-forgive-you fall (Barbara Fusar-Poli and Maurizio Margaglio), and if you want I can go on *ad infinitum* and *ad nauseum.*

A while back I received a Communication from the International Skating Union (ISU), explaining what a fall was. Now, we all thought we knew what a fall was, but this intended to clear up any lack of understanding or misunderstanding that could possibly, by any dint of memory loss or other stupidity, still be harbored somewhere in our tiny little minds.

This communication explained so many different things. What constituted a fall! How much of the body was wherever. What supported the body if it was supported at all, et cetera, et cetera, and also whether it was a fall if only half the buttocks were on the ice and supporting the body.

A short time later, another ISU communication was sent reporting "Clarifications, Changes and Amendments" to the previous communication on falls.

It was indeed fascinating to see that the definition of a fall was finally settled. It is now defined in the Special Regulations and Technical Rules for 2012 (Rule 353, paragraph M, sub (ii) on page 20). Officially, it is a "loss of control by a skater with the result that the majority [but what majority part?] of his/her own body weight [not someone else's?] is on the ice [not, I guess, outside the hockey barrier—Remember Midori Ito jumping through the TV cutout in the hockey barrier at the 1991 World Championship?] supported by any other part of the body other than the blades [are blades a part of the body?] e.g. hand(s), knee(s), back, buttock(s) [If one buttock, can it be either one?] or any part of the arm."

My goodness! This takes some thinking, and I for one certainly don't want to be the one to do the thinking.

As an aside (I continue to love these asides), "deductions will be applied for interruption of the program: -1.0 for 11 to 20 seconds interruption, -2.0 for 21 to 30 seconds interruption etc." (Now, what is the "etc." for? Further lengths of time? Or some other part of the body hitting the ice?)

Sorry, but I hope someone will come by soon and explain the necessity for this type of rule! I guess the judges must all be considered nincompoops because they certainly are removed from most decision making.

However, having said that, I will report on the valiant attempt by the governing body of skating in America, United States Figure Skating (USFS) to attempt to clarify any misunderstanding of the rules.

During the National Championships after the new IJS rules were established, Gale Tanger, a USFS official, was appointed to work with the television crew to answer any questions about the rules.

The subject of falls came up. Gayle, a good-looking, long-legged, ex-dancer and aspiring top honcho at the ISU and USFS, offered to demonstrate what a fall was. The offer was accepted.

Gale got down on the floor and showed everyone the different positions the body could take during a fall. With her body rolling around the carpet, her legs going everywhere as well as up in the air, and sometimes almost like one of those street dancers who can spin on their shoulders, she demonstrated what portions of the body core would be on the ice; what, if anything, was supported by the arm(s); and whether she was on one or both buttocks. Sprawled over the carpet and with all extremities moving like a windmill in a hurricane, she succeeded in creating some of the most alarming positions I have seen.

When the demonstration was concluded, the room

was silent. Then a small voice from the back (*not mine*) asked if she would please do that again.

But please, folks here on the couch with me, remember that falls can cause truly dangerous head injuries, and that they must be treated immediately and with the best care possible.

At the 2000 World Figure Skating Championships at the Palais des Expositions in Nice, the pair skaters Julia Obertas and Dmitri Palamarchuk were doing an overhead lift when he caught an edge and fell. She fell on top of him. He lay on the ice and did not move. (Later he was taken to a hospital, where it was determined that he had not suffered any serious damage.) It did cause the withdrawal of the pair. But what concerned me was that as he lay on the ice, helpers from backstage ran out on the ice. Lifting him up to a standing position, one of them started slapping his face back and forth to bring him to. I am afraid I went berserk calling out to stop slapping his head back and forth. No one seemed to consider the situation; Ottavio Cinquanta, the president of the ISU, was busy talking to Prince Albert of Monaco and not watching. The helpers walked Dmitri off the ice.

The point of this is every championship must have accredited medical support at hand (which I understand is now the case), and unknowledgeable helpers, even well-meaning ones, should not be allowed around an injured skater.

I tell this story also because I had a major head injury. On the last day of 2000, I went ice skating. I knew I would be going out that night to celebrate the New Year and would probably indulge myself, so a little exercise was welcome. On the ice I was at first stiff and moved haltingly. But then the endorphins began to kick in, and I felt the juices returning. I thought maybe I could try something more difficult. I don't remember what it was for sure, but I suspect it was an Axel—that forward-edge, most dangerous of all jumps (dangerous because as I mentioned in chapter 7, the forward edge can shoot away at any second and one can go Flop! Flop! Splat!)

Whatever it was that I tried was something I had done a thousand times and certainly knew how to do. My body also knew perfectly well how to do it. The problem was, my body did not do it fast enough. It was like those small miscalculations that make you misjudge and trip on a step and go *bump*—which happens as one gains "maturity."

After I fell and with blood on my head and face, I nevertheless insisted on going to the party that was scheduled. When told I was being taken to the emergency room instead, I hauled off and hit my friend Dennis Grimaldi, who had been alerted to what had happened. An ambulance took me to a local hospital, where a friendly nurse advised to him to get me to a Brain Trauma Center. I was flown by helicopter to the closest one (in White Plains, New York).

I remember little of the next few weeks. I was in a straitjacket, which was needed to restrain me. Shortly after, I developed meningitis, and it was touch and go for a while. Then I was in rehab for three months. It took a year to accomplish the repairs that were need to recuperate from a fracture, a concussion, the loss of hearing in my left ear, and various other problems too numerous to recite.

The rehab process was a major hurdle for my family and those around me.

I worked hard to recover. I refused to listen when told I would never balance a checkbook, let alone balance on skates again. When I finally got my act together, I became a spokesperson for the Brain Injury Association of America. It was an enlightening experience, speaking on the subject of how a family reacts to someone severely injured and the difficulties they face with caring for that person.

Almost a year after my injury, I was scheduled to make a short speech at a skating exhibition in Madison Square Garden. I remember walking out to the stage and passing Olympic skating champion Hayes Jenkins and whispering, "I don't know if I can make this."

In the center of the stage and in order to gain balance, I planted my feet far apart and spread my toes wide in my shoes as the therapist had taught me. Then I gave the speech, which I had endlessly rehearsed. I made one small misstep and then walked off past Hayes. He said, "You did just fine, Dick."

I was lucky in that I seem to have suffered few permanent damages, as the result of my fall (others may argue with this!). Both Dmitri Palamarchuk and I were lucky. The pair skater Paul Binnebose, who had suffered a major fall during training in 1999, suffered some permanent issues. He is today teaching and functioning happily and well.

The falls these skaters took raised the subject of whether skaters, particularly pair skaters, should wear helmets. Bikers should always wear protection, as pebbles and ruts can cause trouble even for experienced riders. Skaters, on the other hand, create programs where costume, music, and performance are paramount, and a helmet would mar the whole picture. The use of helmets has been minimal except in practice, but the audience as well as those skating to *Carmen* or some other romantic concept would find it disconcerting in performance. A helmet over the white feathers of a "swan" on a "lake" wouldn't work too well.

The practice of wearing protective gear never got going. And falls—bumps, bumbles, and tumbles—continue to be an occupational hazard for skaters.

Falls also elicit a variety of reactions. Some in the audience may see falls as part of the event. Sometimes a performer takes a fall more seriously (meaning they are losing more than their pride). And some in an audience will admire the resilience of a skater and their ability to pick themselves up, dust themselves off, and keep going—which they then applaud. Sometimes there is a morbid sense of anticipation among some folk who like scary movies and who wait for the unexpected to shatter the calm. I suspect that for them there is not much enthusiasm for yet another fall on a triple or quadruple jump, which seems to occur every other second and therefore has become boring.

So how does the skater, and how do we, look at these mishaps? I guess what it all boils down to is that the skater must be prepared to pick themselves up, dust themselves off, and . . . well, doesn't everyone know the drill by now?

9 TO WILT, OR NOT TO WILT?

Most of us don't face moments like those an Olympic skater faces. For example, there's that moment when the pressure is frightening and years of work culminate in one performance that lasts only a few minutes. It is then that the soufflé must souffel! If it doesn't, the effort comes screeching to a halt.

How does one best prepare for that moment? One's personal experience may be the best guide to start with. (Sorry! "may be the best guide with which to start"! Shades of Winston Churchill and "Up with this I will not put"!)

At age twelve or so, I was enrolled in a very small boys' day school in Englewood, New Jersey. It was rightly called the Englewood School for Boys but has since that time become grander than it was by joining with the girls' school next door called the Dwight School for Girls (presumably for Ladies of Gentle Birth and Upbringing, a phrase I may have used elsewhere in our couch conversation in reference to ladies and their skating costumes—or lack thereof!). It is now the Dwight-Englewood School.

But before its elevation to this combined social opportunity, classes were segregated. The boys' classes were held in the carriage house behind a large, forbidding, dark gray, late Victorian house.

All the boys tried to play games as much as possible, and in one of the classes on English Literature, much time was spent making jokes and puns on Shakespeare's most famous lines.

Thus Hamlet's famous line, "To be, or not to be: that is the question" became "To cough, or not to cough? Consumption be the congestion." And a line from *Twelfth Night* when Sebastian said to Antonio, "I can no other answer make than thanks, and thanks, and ever thanks" became, "I can no udder answer make than tanks, and tanks, and ever tanks."

Yes, it was sophomoric! But many of us are sophomoric and are a lot older than thirteen.

I began skating in competition at thirteen, and the reason I was sent to this school was because it was small enough to accommodate my desire to compete in skating championships. A larger school like Choate was not possible because there were too many students to allow for the special, peculiar needs of any one student. (My oldest brother George had "gone away," as it was called, to Choate, and my next older brother, Jack, went away to Choate, too—and also to every other school on the eastern seaboard, always getting kicked out of each (he relishes telling everyone that!).

When I needed to take a week off to go to the 1943 Eastern States Novice Men's competition, my parents made me ask the headmaster for permission. He had the marvelous name of Marshall Umpleby. He looked the part of the perfect headmaster at a small boys' school with a bow tie and worn tweed jacket with leather patches on the elbows. When he heard I was asking for a week off to compete in a figure skating competition, he thought for only a second, and then, to his great credit, he did not say no, but instead asked his secretary to show him my grades. All students took six courses. A grade of 60 was passing. I had five 60s and one 61. Mr. Umpleby said calmly and quietly, "You want a week off? I want 70s." He got the 70s, and I got the week off.

Then I learned still another variation on Mr. Shakespeare's masterpiece. "To be, or not to be" became "To wilt, or not to wilt. Can falling be the Matterhorn? Don't sitz, don't sitz."

(Sorry, but didn't I warn you at the beginning?)

This is a very long story just to tell you that the cry "Not to wilt!" has been a major theme in my life ever since.

In those earlier days of skating, a coach accompanied us to competitions, and sometimes a parent went also. Today, every skater who shows promise probably has not only a coach and at least one parent but also a choreographer, physical trainer, an agent, and a sports psychologist.

We learned to deal with pressure by learning what we thought was a solid skating technique, which fostered a feeling of security. We had been taught (and trained long and hard enough) to know where each part of the body should be at each moment of the jump or spin, or any other moment in the program. Of course, the operative words here were "a solid technique." Gustave Lussi had been a ski jumper and understood both flight and rotation.

In addition, he had an analytical mind, dissected everything, and broke every movement down into component parts.

No one thought of "imagining" that we would win. Nor did we "visualize" the program. It was, instead, a matter of remembering a specific position for each move. Gustave Lussi had taught us multiple positions for each move (shoulder levels; head, leg and arm positions; the lean of the body; et cetera). By the time competition came around, these had been culled down to remembering one specific position that would simplify yet focus our concentration and ignite total muscle memory.

Many today use sports psychiatry, which can be extremely helpful. It is just that we never were taught it in any formal way. I never felt the need to go into a bathroom stall like Brian Boitano did, close the door, and sit on the john while wearing headphones to listen to music to keep the noise out. (I must remember to ask him what it was he was listening to.) Whatever it was, he skated his best in Calgary, Canada, at the 1988 Olympic Winter Games and won the gold medal.

Everyone needs their own special preparation for doing their best. Doing your best is the name of the game when you are in the Olympics—or, for that matter, anywhere else.

In addition, we learned two extremely important things:

1. "hold back" for the first thirty seconds in the Free Skating program.
2. "Skate for six days and take the seventh day off."

Many of us were like racehorses at the gate straining to charge onto the racecourse. Or into the sunset! That was dangerous, and Gustave Lussi knew that the need was to hold us back and not let us "leave the title at the starting gate" by messing up in the first thirty seconds.

It was common for a group of us to play a game when we watched the novice or junior events. The rules of our game called for stating within five seconds of the start of a program whether the skater would fall in the first thirty seconds. Did the skater blast off, already out of control? Most of the time we could easily pick the ones who would fall.

In 1945, The National Championships took place at the New York Skating Club on the fourth floor of the old Madison Square Garden. I competed in the Men's Junior event. For the first time, I was leading in the Compulsory Figures portion of the competition by some sixty points, an almost unbeatable lead. But I had set out to show all and sundry that here was one "Dickie" (I hated that moniker) Button coming down the pike by giving the best performance I could. One of the first jumps was a double loop. I attacked it but never got off the ice. The edge I was on went out and I went down. Shortly thereafter I landed a double flip on two knees, sliding into the barrier. I pulled myself up and did not even see my father's face, which was two feet in front of me, I was that out of control.

At the end of the program and after making other major mistakes and still out of control, I skated off the ice and walked down the four flights of concrete steps to 52nd Street without putting my guards on, ruining my blades as I ground them into the steel steps and the concrete of the sidewalk.

Gustave Lussi caught up with me and, controlling his anger, told me that I had just one more chance not to "leave it all at the starting gate."

I call that "wilting," which can happen at any time, not just at the start of the program. There is nothing more disheartening than to see a truly talented skater put on a performance that is breathtaking, performing superbly in move after move—and then trip.

I've seen competitors miss jumps they have done time and time again and could do with one hand tied behind their back. Legions of skaters have fallen into this trap.

But don't let me sound pompous (yet again!), because I fell into that very trap. It happened in one of the most important competitions of all.

In 1952, at age twenty-two, I made the team for the Olympic Winter Games in Oslo. I was now a senior at Harvard and being urged to go on to law school (when what I really wanted was to skate and be involved in the theater!).

In those days there was no income from skating. A present for an exhibition was limited to $25. The Skating Club of Boston had given me a pair of silver hairbrushes for an exhibition, which meant a great deal then and still does today, even though I lost my hair. Nor were there scholarships for skating expenses, and it was time I started thinking of other things besides skating. Many of the new skaters were fourteen to seventeen years old and I felt *muchly* superior. After all, I was now twenty-two, a world traveler, about to be a college graduate, and had been written about in *Life* magazine. I was, I thought, no longer a member of the hoi polloi—oy!

It was time to move on. But the Olympics were coming up, and I wanted more than anything to give the best performance I possibly could. It was my senior year. I dropped all extracurricular activities, took early courses over the summer, and prepared for an extensive training program. We scheduled a long period of training time in the winter in Garmisch-Partenkirchen, south of Munich, Germany.

I got into the best shape of my life.

We moved on to Oslo. There had been no Olympic Village in St. Moritz in 1948 due to the end of World War II; we stayed in hotels. In Oslo in 1952 there was an Olympic Village, but my parents felt I needed to stay in a hotel in central Oslo where I could get sufficient sleep and not be distracted by the exuberant goings-on of young athletes.

It was the worst decision we could have made.

I can test my hindsight against your foresight any day of the week! Looking back now, I realize what happened: neither Gustave Lussi nor I remembered to put in place the second of his two teachings: "Skate for six days and take the seventh day off."

When I arrived in Oslo, the first practice, five days before the competition, was the most satisfying skating session I had ever had. I had trained diligently and was in the best of condition. My body simply did everything I asked it to do. I still remember the sensation, and no palimpsest will ever dim that.

But the next day the session had dropped a peg. I

kept pushing and the next three sessions were also each down another peg. Still I kept trying to repeat the first day's success.

The problem may have been at least in part because I was not staying at the Olympic Village where the fun and action was. Instead, at the hotel, dinner was with my parents and Gustave Lussi. I loved them all. They were great in every way, but they were not a bundle of joking buddies. In fact, there was a tautness in my world that was close to snapping. I should have been romping around with others who were having the same highs and lows and discovering maybe, just maybe, that it was not going to be the end of the world if I didn't skate well. (Who am I kidding?)

My roommate from Harvard, one Aldus Higgins Chapin, believing that I had a chance to win an Olympic gold medal and that he probably would never have another roommate in such a position, decided to fly over and see what was happening. But neither he nor I could get out on the town. And in Oslo and during Olympic week, there was not much "on the town" except at the Olympic Village.

Sure enough, in the competition I made mistakes. At these games I was a much better skater than I had been at the 1948 Olympic Games. But at that event I skated the best I could. At the 1952 Games, I did not skate the best I could.

Even though I was able to be the first to do a triple jump (it was a triple loop), it was not for me a satisfying championship. In fact, to be truthful, I still smart at the stupid mistakes I made. I won, but it was not perfect. It was not the best I could do.

A few days later, we had lunch in Oslo at the home of friends of my family. They lived in a large, 200-year-old house. The family had three daughters who served the entire lunch on one huge silver platter in the central room of the house where we were seated. The room was double height and the walls were lined with ancient wooden paneling. It was an exceedingly pleasant afternoon, and the conversation flowed.

Until, that is, I realized that I was scheduled to skate an exhibition (as is usually done at the end of the Olympic Games)—and that I had forgotten it was that afternoon. I had no time to practice or warm up. Overfed and not warmed up, I nevertheless skated as well as I had hoped to do in the competition.

What was going on?

(There's a point to this long story, so please hang in there!)

A day later, we took the train to Paris. The 1952 World Championships were scheduled for ten days later. My parents, Gus Lussi, and I were housed in the Claridge's Hotel on the Champs-Élysées, an elegant but very tired old hotel since converted to offices. Aldie Chapin was still with us (no point in missing Paris!). And we didn't. We were doing everything folks could do in Paris when they're twenty-two.

And we weren't getting back to the hotel 'til very late.

My father who could be Germanic (even though he was of English extraction) huffed and puffed, saying, "This is a World Championship" and I shouldn't stay out late. I needed "to train."

My mother looked him straight in the eye and said, "George, you are absolutely right!" Then, looking at me, she said, "Dick, your father is right. Get back early." Then she proceeded to shake hands with me, and secreted in the palm of her hand was a bunch of francs!

Aren't mothers great?

I skated well in that championship.

Years later, I realized how important this lesson was.

At the Neighborhood Playhouse in New York City, I was studying acting with Sanford Meisner, one of the forces of The Actors Studio (Marlon Brando, James Dean, Marilyn Monroe, and the rest of those guys), and one of the best lessons he gave was all about the strength of preparation you needed to undertake a role. He would clench his fist to demonstrate the power and force of character needed. But then he'd say, "You also need to encase it in relaxation," and with that he would place the open palm of his other hand over the fist.

His point was clear. Strength was necessary for performance, but not sufficient by itself. One needed to combine it with relaxation. Only then were you were ready to go.

I combined the strength of the training I had done all winter with the relaxation of Paris.

Having done that, I skated well in Paris!

As another of my beloved asides, recall the 1998 Olympic Winter Games in Nagano. Michelle Kwan was the favorite in the women's figure skating competition. She was staying not at the Olympic Village, but with her parents and her agent at the same slightly dull (?) Holiday Inn as I was. How's that for a group of comedians for dinner partners? (Actually, Mr. Kwan and I always have a good laugh together about things. But . . . Shades of Oslo?)

Tara Lipinski, the fifteen-year-old sprite, also from the United States, was challenging her. Tara was staying at the Olympic Village and was running around seeing and greeting everyone. She was five foot one and was playing ping-pong with six foot four athletes from everywhere. She was having the time of her life.

It seemed she had nothing to lose, skated her heart out, and won.

This is not to say that if Michelle had been staying at the Olympic Village, she would have won! It is just to draw awareness toward what might have been a similar situation to mine.

The best-laid plans can all too often go awry!

It also made me laugh when Paul Wylie (the U.S. Champion and subsequent winner of the silver medal at the 1992 Olympic Winter Games in Albertville) was assigned to room with Christopher Bowman, a two-time national champion. Bowman was a charismatic, highly talented, skater who dazzled audiences consistently—as well as every girl in sight.

He came swinging into the dormitory room at 5:00 in the morning when Paul was still asleep and started joking and bouncing on the bed. That was enough to make either or both of them wilt. Paul did not wilt. He skated brilliantly.

Paul told me, "Every mother wanted the girls to go out with me, while every girl wanted to go out with Christopher."

So as we start on a big slice of pizza (and another round of beer), it will be interesting to watch the preparation of the skaters as they take the ice. What presence do they show? What attitude do they have? Most important is seeing whether a skater will "wilt or not wilt."

In my day there were multiple things that could impede and distract a skater. In the United States in the 1940s, we skated mostly indoors at places like the Philadelphia Skating Club and Humane Society (I will explain about the "Humane Society" at a another trip to the bar) or in Lake Placid at the Olympic Arena built for the 1932 Olympic Winter Games where Sonja Henie won the second of her three Olympic titles. The point is, we were mostly indoors and under controlled situations. But at the 1947 World Championships in Stockholm, the first World Championships following World War II, the competition was outdoors.

I was not accustomed to outdoor ice. The weather was not something you could describe with just one word. It included sharp sunlight, overcast skies, clouds, rain, changing direction of the wind, varying temperatures, slush, bitterly cold ice, and myriad other conditions.

There were any number of factors to be aware of. How was the ice made? What happened when the sun went down over the mountains and a crust formed over slush? What about the effects of wind and rain and melted ice? Anything could and did happen. Even the music could play at a questionable speed when the needle was dropped on your 75 rpm record, or the speed varied. Or the record itself was dropped—and did you have a second, third, or fourth copy with you, or were you destined to skate to the Swedish national anthem? And who was playing the record? In 1947 in Stockholm, Gustave Lussi went over to where the record player was to make sure that the record was put on with care and that the speed was right. He needn't have worried—the hulking six foot seven Swede in charge was indeed *in charge* and all was OK. But could you be sure?

And what about travel? Transatlantic flight was just coming into regular use back then, and my father had always traveled by boat during the 1930s. So to get to Stockholm in 1947, we first took the Queen Mary, a transatlantic ocean liner, to Southampton and then the boat train to London. There, after five days on the high seas, we were scheduled to skate.

But the rocking of the boat (and the seasickness it caused most folks) left one feeling unbalanced. Yet in London it was skate we must! It was the first time we had seen any other skaters in Europe, and the first time they had seen us.

It was an unnerving moment. The most we could muster was a sit spin. But it was reported by spectators as being acceptable!

The next boat trip from London to Stockholm was still another two days at sea, and the North Sea was also blessed with heavily rolling waves. It was enough to make anyone wilt.

In Stockholm, I had no idea how to skate figures on outdoor ice in temperatures that were below zero. The most prominent skater from Europe was Hans Gerschweiler of Switzerland. He had grown up skating on outdoor ice and knew everything about it. What did we

99

hothouse flowers from America know about almost-Arctic temperatures that changed for the better and then for the worse and then back again in a matter of hours or even minutes? What does one do when the temperature drops well below zero and the ice is brittle, splitting off into slivers, leaving you in deep canyons of ice?

The problem happened on a figure called a loop change loop. Most figures were made of circles, where each circle usually was three times the size of the skater (fifteen to seventeen feet, more or less). A loop, however, referred to a smaller circle approximately the size of the skater (five to six feet) with a still smaller loop (approximately one foot) inside. This meant that the edges into the smallest loop were tighter and in brittle ice, your skates could cut down into deep canyons, chipping away the ice and wreaking havoc with both the figure and the skater.

Hans won the figures handily, and I was lucky to come in second.

Back in Lake Placid, I spent a season training outdoors at the Lake Placid Club tennis courts to learn every nuance of what outdoor ice was all about. What direction did the light come from? Were you skating the figure going into the light or with the light behind you so you could see the other side of your figures? How did you place your figure? What direction was the wind coming from? Was it blowing straight into your face? Or did it come from behind you, pushing you along on the slow, last part of the figure? What happened after the sun went down behind the mountain and left a sliver of hard ice over a half-inch of slush? What happened when the temperature was bitterly cold? Did you use an older pair of skates with leather boots that were well-worn and softer than your free skating boots, so the knee could bend more easily into the tight edges, particularly those of a loop figure?

Skating outdoors took getting used to the layer of air

under outdoor ice if it was on a pond or lake. That space gives the ice an elasticity that would give a spring to your jumps. None of that is present in today's World Arenas, where the ice is almost always the same: hard, "dead" ice over concrete.

That was why one wore sweaters (that your mother had knitted with Native American motifs or skaters doing split jumps across your chest). And why you carried three pairs of skates when you eventually took airplanes to fly "across the Pond" so no important luggage could be accidentally sent to another city. You could skate in your long johns if you had to (come to think of it, at that time there was no rule to prevent it—and some of us may remember that when the Shipstads and Johnson started Ice Follies and didn't have enough money for costumes, they sewed up long johns and attached sequins—and it worked!). But you needed to have skating boots, particularly ones that were broken in for figures.

Any number of problems such as these might upset the apple cart and cause you to wilt.

But then the ice could also be magical, as it was at the Suvretta House (a hotel in St. Moritz where the Shah of Iran stayed, as did a host of glamorous beauties). All of the hotels in St. Moritz at that time had skating rinks that were for the guests of the hotel. There the fellows who tended the rink knew how to make ice that was like velvet. When you did figures or free skated on that kind of ice, it was like carving your blades into soft butter.

A month before the 1948 Olympics, the European Championships were held in the Zimni Stadion, a roofless rink on an island in the Moldau River in the center of Prague.

The weather was poor and the soft wind that blew down the river and over the rink warmed the ice and melted it. There was water everywhere, and no one could see a figure that was skated. There was little to judge except positions and style, and Hans Gerschwiler and I were closely tied. I won on the free skating and was thus the only American ever to win the European Championship. Barbara Ann Scott of Canada won the ladies' event, and the International Skating Union then closed the event to non-Europeans.

(As a slightly off-center aside, I truly enjoy tweaking Scott Hamilton with the fact that I am the *only* American who could win this competition. I never add why as he could have won it handily!)

A month later in St. Moritz at the Winter Olympic Games, the figures were held on the ice rink at the Kulm Hotel. The ice was like velvet. My year-long exertions to understand outdoor ice were to no immediate avail. It was, however, a fascinating study.

It was a different time and a different world. Now there are no figures. There are no more of those intricate elaborate drawings done by us folks, which we spent as much as five hours a day learning to do. No wonder others thought we were insane. Now the world of figure skating has eliminated those elaborate concoctions that took several hundred years to create, and we find ourselves in yet another insane world where instant messaging about every thing we might have eaten at lunch seems paramount. I sometimes wonder whether we were the lucky ones to have known this strange, magical, lost world!

But one thing is constant in the world of skating. Just as then, there are now hundreds of things that can distract you and make you wilt.

Perhaps it is time to consider just what "to wilt" means. It is broader than just referring to a skater who falls. There are so many ways to wilt besides falling. My lack of knowledge about outdoor ice and the effect of skating on that brittle ice in the 1947 World Championships in Stockholm made me wilt. At the National Junior Championships when I wilted and fell twice, it was due to my failure to "hold back." Sasha Cohen many times would come close to the end of an exquisite program, completing all the difficult jumps, and then out of the blue would trip, spoiling the total picture. Was this a failure to retain concentration, or what? It is necessary to question why Patrick Chan, who skated a phenomenal Short Program at the 2013 World Championships, then wilted in the Long Program. His mistakes and misses in the Long Program were shocking, even though he won the title. What was the cause of his wilting?

However, we all have to remember that even the best of us can wilt. The real question is, can we learn to deal with our mistakes, address the problem, and find a solution to it? Living with repeated failures, particularly small ones, is not a good alternative to figuring out how to cope with them. We should not let "the wilt factor" become a pattern. Sometimes only we can figure out the solution.

It is also a matter of our attitude. Can we ride above the problem and put it aside? In the 1984 Olympic Games, Barbara Underhill and Paul Martini were in a leading position to win the gold medal. They were powerful, superb pair skaters who had consistently skated with security. Yet in this event, Barbara stepped into a pair sit spin, lost the entering hook needed to center the spin (remember the "Camel Club" split chin story in chapter 6 on centering?), and slid into and knocked down Paul Martini. Whether it was anxiousness, the speed of the entrance, the failure to concentrate on the "hook" that would have centered her spin, or something else, we will never know. The point here is Barbara Underhill, one of the finest skaters ever, had done this move too many times to count, and was experienced in competitions. Those of us watching will never know the reason for that wilt of the moment. However, when I spoke to her about this and commiserated with her on the loss of the gold, she replied that if they had won, they would have turned professional immediately and thus they would have lost the heartwarming celebration when they won the World Championships the following year in their home country. Talk about coping with a mishap! This was the way to handle it.

I only know that in my own competitions, I remember always saying to myself toward the end of the program, "Hold on, hold on!" It was my very amateurish means of forcing continued concentration and for me it was fairly effective. And that is ultimately a skater's best weapon against wilting or continuing to wilt: finding the unique thing, or combination of things, that will keep that particular skater's mind and body attuned, relaxed, and ready for anything. Because on ice, anything goes—and usually does!

Me doing a change loop, showing the
precise tight edging figures needed.

Mom, Dad, and me onboard the Queen Mary on
the way to the 1948 Olympics in St. Moritz.

The 1948 U.S. Olympic team in St. Moritz.

The teacher who taught me everything, Gustave Lussi.

1948 Olympic Champions, Canadian Barbara Ann Scott
and me, in St. Moritz.

Me doing an inside spread eagle on
Mirror Lake in Lake Placid.

Me doing a flying sit spin on Mirror Lake, Lake Placid.
Flying sit spins were prized moves back then.

Ulrich Salchow in a signed photo he gave me in 1947.

Me wearing tights in the early 1940's. There wasn't
much change since Ulrich Salcow's day, but
it certainly changed later.

The 1901 trophy that Ulrich Salchow gave me,
that I gave to John Misha Petkevich,
who gave it to Paul Wylie.

Belita Jepson-Turner, 1936 Olympian, ballerina, actress, stage and movie star (*Suspense*), showing extraordinary stretch and pointed feet.

Pierre Brunet and Andrée Joly, 1928 and 1932 Olympic Pair Champions, in an elegant Art Deco style pair spiral.

Soviet Leader Nikita Khrushchev, me, and the
cast of Holiday on Ice in Moscow.

The Domes of Red Square had almost as much movement
as the arms of skaters do in todays new IJS rules.

Tab Hunter and me doing stag jumps during the rehearsals
for the TV special *Hallmark Hall of Fame:*
Hans Brinker of The Silver Skates.
Photo credit: From the collection of Tab Hunter

My early days on TV. Is that a hairpiece or not?

Jim McKay and me doing on-ice intros at the
1962 World Figure Skating Championships in Prague.

Jim McKay and me in our usual tuxedos.

I always took my job as expert commentator
very seriously…

...most of the time, that is.

The Superstars was fun, too!

119

The 1984 World Professional Championships.

Aja Zanova, Czech and World Champion, in
Ice Capades in a dazzling hybrid split jump.

Janet Lynn in Ice Follies, showing superb
position and the joy of skating.

Doing a Russian split jump in Central Park, New York.

I finally learned to stretch! A Mazurka
jump in Central Park, New York.

Me doing a camel spin later in life! In my day, boys did not do camel spins. I did it first in competition by doing a so-called "military position" with arms on the legs. The Button or Flying Camel came later.

Peggy Fleming, Terry Gannon, and me. I'm wearing my Harvard "H" in a Yale quad. We were in New Haven for a TV shoot. Please note I could (almost) wear it some 40 years later!

At Skate America 1993 in Dallas, the hosts Julie Moran and Peggy Fleming were off the cuff, off the shoulder, and spectacular too!

1980 Olympics in Lake Placid.

Dorothy Hamill in her iconic wedge haircut and glasses
and me in the hated yellow ABC jackets. 1980 Olympics in
Lake Placid.

Brian Boitano doing one great spread eagle with the
flattest back—and it's an outside edge one, too!
Photo credit: Jay Adeff

Peggy and me in St. Petersburg for the Goodwill Games in the summer of 1994. We should have stood aside to show you the bronze statue of Oleg Protopopov and Ludmila Belousova, erected after the Wall came down and the Russian government finally recognized them for their accomplishments.

Michelle Kwan and me at the 1998 Olympics in Nagano.

Many of the US Olympic Champions at the showing of
the documentary *Rise*.

Dorothy Hamill and me at the
2010 Olympics in Vancouver.

Cerrito and Carlotta, who are on the couch with you
during this "conversation."

This photo is on the piano next to the couch where you are sitting. It is of my children, Emily and Edward, on their first day of school.

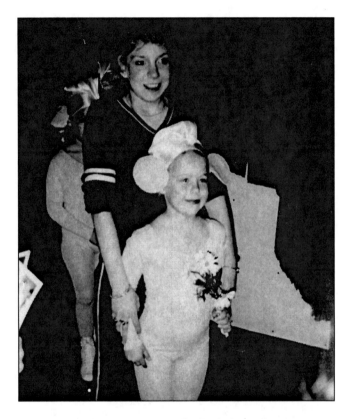

Like Elaine Zayak, Emily liked show skating.

The best kind of ice, black ice, at Ice Pond Farm.

It wasn't all work! Peggy and me in Russia.
Photo credit: From the collection of Peggy Fleming

10 A REQUEST! AND A FEW COMMENTS ON COMMENTARY

Having been an expert (?) on-air commentator myself, I listen carefully to what other commentators say and also to what the directors cover and what the general tone of the event is.

They have interesting remarks that, most of the time, advance our knowledge (if we ignore statements of the obvious, such as, "he fell").

But there are two words or phrases often used that I hope I never, ever, ever say.

One is: "AMAAAAAAAAAAAZING!"

The other is: "He [or she] NAILED it!"

Neither contains the slightest imagination or information in describing the moment. "Amaaaazing" is the sort of lightweight adjective frequently heard in "red carpet" interviews with the flavor-of-the-month starlet.

And "he nailed it" always makes me think that someone's tongue has been stapled onto the ice (please don't give me a retort on this! I know what you're thinking!).

So if I ever slip and say either of these things in the throes of excitement, I shall personally wash out my mouth with soap. Of course, the operative words here are "in the throes of excitement." Which leads me to grab another handful of popcorn and tell you about the first time I narrated a skating event (sorry to play the Granddaddy role again!).

It was at the 1960 Olympic Winter Games in Squaw Valley. I was working with Bud Palmer, the very popular, well-known, talented, six foot five CBS sports host mainstay. He knew nothing about figure skating and said so. And I knew nothing about commentating and said so. So there was no alternative for the two of us but to just jump in and get started.

I learned several things from Bud. One was to try and not speak too rapidly. The listening public usually could only hear so much at any one time without being distracted by something they were seeing or by taking a "refrigerator break" (Oh my, I mustn't say that again!).

I told Bud that in skating, knowledgeable folk never used the word "twirl" to describe a spin. Nor did they use the word "leap" to describe a jump. David Jenkins (who won the Olympic gold medal at these games) had the softest knees, best edging, and "jump spring" you can imagine, and when he erupted from a deep knee edge into one of the highest, cleanest jumps I had seen, I promptly exploded with, "What a great leap!"

Bud exploded with laughter!

So much for my brilliant advice.

Covering those Games was a learning experience. My contract called for a payment of $2,000 for being the "expert commentator." I tried to learn as fast as I could and constantly called New York to ask all and sundry what they liked (and, more importantly, what they did not like). I made so many calls that my telephone bill was over $3000.

The best piece of advice came from acclaimed

Broadway producer Paul Feigay, who gave me endless comments on the coverage. He said that there was one jump that I was able to talk about before it was done because it had a very long entrance. I knew instantly he was talking about a Lutz jump, which usually signaled its arrival by a long back outside edge.

(Another aside! Don't forget to ask me about those *long* Lutz entrances and how they can create point-getting havoc if you happen to wiggle or wobble a fraction off a perfect and constant edge—known in the trade as a flutz—let alone skate too near the barrier.)

Feigay's comments made me realize that it was interesting for people to be alerted to what the skaters would do *before* they did it. The other choice was always to be left saying, "That 'was' an Axel" after the move was already over and we had visually moved on. So I spent hours tracking down skaters and asking if they would tell me the order of their moves. I asked the coaches, too.

The skaters could, sort of, remember the order of jumps and spins. But I needed to find ways to check by saying, "Don't you do a spread eagle?" The skater would then say, "Oh, yes, it comes after the flip jump" (which they had also forgotten to include).

Frequently the coaches would mix up the order of the moves.

One prominent coach said where his pupil would do a sit spin. In my commentary, I started to talk about what a sit spin was, the best position, who invented it (Jackson Haines), and luckily did not say that it would be done at the start of the program. The skater then did a double Axel. I was left with egg on my face (no, it was not the first time, and certainly not the last!).

It was clear that not only did I have to ask each skater and each coach about the order of the program, but also that I had to see each program in practice. I carefully constructed a list of each skater's major (identifiable) moves.

During my commentary, I found myself needing to follow the moves on the list while also watching the skater on the ice. But it was also necessary to watch the TV monitor because you did not want to talk about something the cameramen might not be showing and that the TV audience was therefore not seeing, and I also needed to listen to what the director was saying through my headphones and also to what the host commentator was saying or had already said. Quadruple trouble! This was multitasking in its purest form. The difference was that nobody used the word multitasking at that time, and any mistakes would be heard by millions of viewers.

The pressure! Oh my! 'Tweren't easy," as the kids say!

This list of moves became known as a "jump sheet." Later, some dingbat skating enthusiast called it a "cheat" sheet. I could happily wring the neck of whomever coined that phrase because it didn't cheat anything, it did nothing more than help alert viewers to look for whatever was coming up, and not have to try to remember seeing what had already been, and it took endless time to create, assemble, and constantly recheck and upgrade. (So don't anyone tell me that person's name! I don't want to know, and besides I have moved on to higher and more elevated thoughts!) (Who are you kidding, Dick?)

Later, jump sheets were compiled for commentators by a "P.A." (a production assistant). Eventually there were untold numbers of production assistants who compiled information of every kind. But at Squaw Valley in 1960 and then in Prague in 1962, it was only us chickens at the trough.

Today, skaters are required early in the season to submit a sequential list of their moves for the Technical Specialists, who note every move (more on this later). If the skater wishes to make changes to that list, he or she needs to resubmit it.

A skater may change an element while actually doing the program. An example would be to change a pre-listed quadruple jump for a jump combination. But skaters who do this must remember what they changed. One can only do a particular jump twice during a program, one of which must be in a combination with another jump. Try making a change in a program you have rehearsed for months while simultaneously thinking through what the rules allow as you attempt to rechoreograph the program on the spot.

This seems highly controlling (but what else is new?).

So much for the "Free" in Free Skating.

The requirement to submit a list of moves is designed to give the Technical Specialists the edge in seeing what is being done and preparing to determine what value it has. But who would require skiers to tell before starting a race which line they would take down the mountain before they knew how the snow was drifting, or how other skiers' ruts had changed the surface, or where the light was coming from, or any other change in conditions occurring at any split second after starting the run?

Look, folks, I know very well that skiers don't get points for their moves on the mountain. It's purely a matter of who stays on the course and crosses the finish line first. *That's* a sport. Is submitting a list and counting the value of each and every move including but not limited to jumps and spins what we get for the honchos wanting the Fine Art of Figure Skating to be considered a sport?! Another example of why Free Skating is not "Free."

Do not think for one moment that being an expert commentator cannot be subject to a whole mess of sinkholes that one can easily fall into.

I found out early about "truthful" critiquing (truthful critiquing was saying what you believed and not making a comment based on an extraneous reason such as rooting for skaters because they were from your own country and not supporting other skaters who you knew were better).

The first time I felt the fury that was possible was during the 1962 World Figure Skating Championships in Prague. The event had been canceled the year before by the International Skating Union out of respect for the U.S. Team members that had been lost in a plane crash. It was one of the greatest tragedies to occur in sports history.

I had purchased the TV rights from the organizing officials in Prague and was finally able to convince ABC to schedule it for *Wide World of Sports*. It had taken two years to convince Roone Arledge that it would be viable programming. (I used to sit on Roone's doorstep, so to speak, constantly monitoring his reactions to what was what in the world of skating and TV programming.)

As an aside, that championship turned out to be one of the most emotional, extraordinary, and impactful skating events I have seen and I am deeply honored to have been part of its history.

First, it had enormous emotional impact because of the death of so many prominent skaters, officials, judges, coaches, and friends on the plane that crashed en route to Prague for the same championship the year before.

Second, it was one of the first sports program to be televised behind the "Iron Curtain," which, as everyone remembers, was the name Winston Churchill gave in a 1946 speech in Fulton, Missouri to the profound gulf in ideology separating the "East" and the "West."

Third: It had the most exciting stories connected to it.

Otto and Maria Jelinek had left Prague with their parents, settling in Canada when the Russians took over Czechoslovakia. They were scheduled to compete as members of the Canadian team in the pair skating event. According to Czechoslovakian law, every male citizen was required to serve in the army, and any male who had fled the country was still considered to be a citizen and subject to army subscription, and in their view this applied to Otto Jelinek. The ISU said, in essence, "Not so, boys; the Jelineks are both Canadian and represent Canada in this event, and if you insist, we will move the event to another country." (Good for them!) The law was exempted for this case, but the government retaliated by never mentioning the Jelineks' names, not listing them or recognizing that they were there, and not allowing the newspapers to print their name.

But guess what? Everyone in Prague knew their story and that they were there.

During every practice session, people came and constantly chanted their name. "Jelinek! Jelinek! Jelinek!" and stomped their feet in time with their chanting. The Jelineks won the World Pair Championship title, and the city went berserk for them.

Fourth: It was the first confrontation between two powerful pairs. Ludmila Belousova and Oleg Protopopov of the Soviet Union (Russia) were classical perfectionists. (They were later to win four World Championships and two Olympic gold medals.) Marika Kilius and Hans-Jürgen Bäumler were good-looking "skating rock stars" from West Germany. They were later to win two World Championships. This was not only a battle of skating styles, but also a confrontation of political ideologies.

Fifth: Don Jackson of Canada became a superhero, doing the first triple Lutz and coming from miles behind in the Figures portion of the men's competition to win over Karel Divin of Czechoslovakia.

Sixth (and finally): The U.S. Men's Champion, seventeen-year-old Monty Hoyt of Denver, Colorado, led the American team, which had been decimated by the plane crash. But right behind him was twelve-year-old Scott Ethan Allen of New York, who became the story of the event as "The Twelve-Year-Old on Whose Small Shoulders the Hopes of the U.S. Rest."

It was this story, one based on an "extraneous reason," that caused the problem for me.

Monty Hoyt's mother, the wife of the editor of *The Denver Post*, was furious that the TV program would show twelve-year-old Scott Allen and not Monty, the U.S. Men's Champion, who was a tall, lanky young man. But "the story" was Scott. As the "rights owner" of the event and also the "expert commentator," the blame was easily placed on me. Scott was from The New York Skating Club and lived in New Jersey. I lived in New York and was from New Jersey. I was accused of favoritism. In the meantime, Mrs. Hoyt, as only an aggrieved mother can do, burst into the hotel room of F. Ritter Shumway, the head of the U.S. skating delegation and, grabbing his shirt (which fistful also included the hair on his chest) demanded he make sure that Monty was included on the program. This left the distinguished Mr. Shumway, a gentleman of the old school, pleading, "Get that woman out of my room."

I also realized at this championship that ABC Sports was interested in "the story" more than anything else. (Food for thought for the current world of skating leaders!)

Television wanted either the most interesting story (young Scott Allen), the most spectacular performance, or the worst one where someone crashed, preferably in a spectacular manner. Thus the opening title sequence of *Wide World of Sports* eventually included the line "the thrill of victory and the agony of defeat," showing for "defeat" a ski jumper by the marvelous name (at least for the American ear) of Vinko Bogataj crashing over the side of the ski jump.

(To misquote my favorite phrase, "There was certainly no jump in that jump"!)

Vinko's mess-up was a stunning *sitzplatz* that became an iconic theme of failure.

Later, I was faced with another accusation of "favoritism" when I cheered the Protopopovs as a pair that transcended the level of pair skating, bringing classical perfection to the Fine Art of Figure Skating. That resulted in a cry that I was "anti-American," and in that difficult time of international confrontation between the U.S. and the Soviet Union, my action was considered by a few zealots as almost traitorous.

Still later, in the battle between Janet Lynn of the U.S.

and Karen Magnusson of Canada, I was loudly criticized for being pro-American and anti-Canadian, despite my unreserved support for so many Canadian skaters, including Barbara Ann Scott, Dafoe and Bowden, Suzanne Morrow, Don Jackson, the Jelineks, Petra Burka, pair champions Bob Paul and Barbara Wagner, and many others.

Finally I pleaded, "Will folks please make up their minds whether I am pro-east coast, pro-west coast, pro-American, pro-Canadian, pro-Russian," or pro whomever the current flavor of the season was.

The truth is, I've always admired a great skater over everything.

A great skater is defined as someone who not only reaches the top but who also leaves the Fine Art of Figure Skating different and better just because they were there!

The folks I applauded achieved that!

That was quite an aside (I like "asides" because otherwise something important or funny might not get told even if it is extraneous and has nothing to do with what we're watching while sitting on the couch. Remember, I provide the popcorn!)!

And that brings me to still another aside, which is that no commentator should ever let the microphone get out of his hand when interviewing someone else. Jim McKay taught me this right at the beginning of our multi-year work together. If you do, he said, you may find yourself unable to get it back while the guy holding it spouts off to his heart's content and the fury of the director.

Sorry I got so far aside. Now I can't even remember what the first aside was!

Oh, yes! I remember now! The suits at ABC Sports had decreed that all of their announcers should replace their customary blue blazers with yellow jackets. I did not like wearing muck-colored yellow. 'Tweren't spiffy, in my limited sartorial opinion. So I told Roone Arledge that it was the custom in figure skating for judges to wear tuxedos. It was a formal sport, after all. He believed me. I wore a tux and was locked into the tuxedo look for some 20 years. I got tired of the damn tuxedo look, but it made it easy to know what tie to put on!

So, let's take a different slant (I like "slants;" they're rather like asides. I am not sure what a "slant" is, but then there's a lot I'm not sure about). I had known from years of skating that mishaps can happen to costumes, skates, and the ice. I quickly learned they can happen to commentators, too.

At the tender age of twenty-two, I had already lost too much hair to suit my vanity. Right after graduating from college, I had signed a contract to skate in the Ice Capades before and intermittently during my first year at Harvard Law School. A friend from Harvard during my collegiate days, Stark Hesseltine, who later became a major theatrical agent and discovered many important stars, had dropped in at Madison Square Garden to see a performance. He brought with him a cork, which he blackened with the help of a lit match, and then used it to blacken the bald spots on the back of my head.

By the time I had gotten to my mid-twenties and was skating in assorted NBC and CBS TV Specials and in *Hans Brinker of The Silver Skates*, my head of hair was gone forever. So I had a hairpiece made. It was an extravaganza! I wore it during a six-week engagement in Holiday on Ice when the show went on its first tour behind the Iron Curtain to Moscow in the Soviet Union. There is a photograph of me with costars of Holiday on Ice Arnold Shoda and Joanne Hyldoft, and the Soviet leader Nikita Khrushchev. The leader of the Soviet Union was personable, approachable, and wildly colorful in his political appearances, which included taking his shoes off and slapping the desk with them at the United Nations. But it was my hairpiece that dominated the photograph.

As an off-center aside but of interest to some skaters

new to the scene, I must tell you that being a producer of events can sometimes be as difficult as competing in them. Everyone should learn that the way to make ends meet in the production of ice shows both on and off TV can be difficult. I am referring to the Holiday on Ice tour mentioned above, which was the first time a theatrical tour of ice shows went to Russia. Relations between the countries in 1959 were not friendly, and no one had the opportunity to travel anywhere behind the Iron Curtain. It would be an education and an opportunity I could not miss. I called Morris Chalfen, the producer, and inquired if there was interest in my being on the tour. Mr. Chalfen (that wily goat!) knew I wanted desperately to go. He also knew my fee had been $13,000 a week in the Ice Capades, which I'd skated in during my first year in law school. First, he made me audition to see if I could still skate (that was to butter me up to his being the boss). Then he offered me $300 a week.

I took it.

So he bested me, but guess what? What he didn't know was I would have paid him in order to go. The trip was worth it and was a memorable educational experience for me. I guess I have always felt that when something is worthwhile, one should do it and ignore whether it makes a financial gain. The experience in this case was payment enough, considering the state of world affairs at the time.

Now, my point here is that Mr. Chalfen knew how to make money, as well as how not to spend money. It was a good lesson for when and where to put the funds one has toward what one feels is important.

(Could that be the reason I spent more money on the hairpiece than I earned on the trip? Regardless, the trip was worth it.)

Later, I mistakenly thought it was important that someone trying to be an actor or a "SPORTS COMMENTATOR" (in *capital letters*, please!) should look youthful and like an athlete. So, at great expense to the management, I ordered a smaller, more sensitive one (meaning one that looked less like a carpet in a bordello, let alone an ordinary rug).

But it was always an embarrassment for me to wear it, particularly when I started commentating at the 1960 Olympic Winter Games in Squaw Valley. At one point, later and in some other event, I was asked to do an ice demonstration that included a "Button Camel" (good boy, Dick!).

The sound engineers taped me up with a microphone that would broadcast my commentary while skating, sending my words to the studio and simultaneously to the audience in the arena.

I was relaxed in the dressing room while they taped my chest tight for the microphone (I was also overweight and out of condition). Then I proceeded to demonstrate a Short Program with the Button Camel at the end. As everyone knows, when doing a Button Camel, you jump from a forward edge over to the other foot as if you're jumping over an imaginary barrel in an open-legged, swan dive-like position, into a back camel spin. When I landed, my head snapped forward, and the hairpiece came unglued and flopped over my face.

My complaining words were two in number, were broadcast to the audience in the arena, and won't be repeated here. I was furious because I knew I would have to do the demonstration over and I was out of breath, out of condition, and tired.

Bud Palmer, meanwhile, was in convulsions, with all six foot plus of his lanky frame stretched over the sports desk. Years later, when Edward, my son, was six years old, he found the hairpiece in the closet. Putting it on his head backwards, he then ran around the house in his underwear. I never wore it again.

Being an expert commentator for so long allowed me to work with some pretty talented hosts (hosts set the scene for the event, announced the marks and what was happening next, and worked with the expert commentator who was the specialist in the sport being covered), starting with Bud Palmer and of course Jim McKay, Chris Schenkel, Al Michaels, Curt Gowdy, Jack Whitaker, the incorrigible Howard Cosell, Bob Costas, Al Trautwig, Keith Jackson, and Terry Gannon, as well as a group of great ladies: Robin Roberts, Leslie Visser, Mary Carillo, and Julie Moran. (Peggy Fleming was a co-commentator, not a host). Julie was probably the tallest at 5'10". She delighted in wearing very high heels, which made me have to look up her nose when we talked. So I brought out a box and stood on it. Julie said she liked being tall. I said I did, too. She took off her stilettos. I took the box away.

A few of the ladies were highly interested in their hair (forget this, Dick; you won't win!). Come to think of it, it wasn't only the ladies. There's a wonderful outtake of Terry Gannon plucking each curl into its right place.

Now, to return to the "request" that started this chapter. I respectfully hope (request?) that the commentators will refrain from talking for the first fifteen seconds at the start of each skater's program. Even though the music is sometimes listed on the TV screen, one should be able to listen to the first few bars to tell whether someone is skating to Beethoven's Fifth, *Carmen*, or some elevator music, or most importantly, what orchestration the skater is using, or how it has been edited!

I know the first move is probably one of the most difficult and valuable point-getters (probably a quadruple, multiple jump combination) but please, please, please keep quiet at the start! You can always get the comment in if it's quick.

At the 2013 World Championships in London, Ontario, I counted the seconds at the start of each of the skaters in the men's events, and all but one took almost thirty seconds to get to that first major jump.

So there should be enough time to hear at least a few strains of the music and still say what the jump will be! Oy!

And speaking of "oy," at the 1980 Olympic Winter Games in Lake Placid, I wound up and gave an impassioned speech about what it meant when pair skater Randy Gardner suffered an injury and had to withdraw. He and Tai Babilonia were going head to head against Irina Rodnina and Alexander Zaitsev of the Soviet Union. It was a battle of countries and philosophies, the U.S. vs. the Soviet Union, Democracy vs. Communism—and also a battle of styles: Babilonia and Gardner being elegant and emotional while Rodnina and Zaitsev were powerhouses.

Gardner's injury and withdrawal also made me feel for the parents and supporters who had spent years driving the skaters to 5:00am practice sessions, endless sums of money and copious amounts of time, only to have it all disintegrate in front of our eyes.

I said so in an impassioned tirade (as I can do best!). Finishing what could be considered a rant, I was silent for a second and then let out an impassioned "*Oy!*" It was a word that summed up the frustration of the moment. What I didn't know was that in the television control truck, Howard Katz, the ABC Sports executive, heard it and as he collapsed in laughter, called out, "That's the quintessential goy calling *oy!*"

I really must continue the search for a more impeccable vocabulary.

11 WHAT IS THE DIFFERENCE BETWEEN THE SHORT PROGRAM AND THE LONG PROGRAM?

Two minutes.

12 WHAT DO YOU MEAN, THERE'S NO DIFFERENCE BETWEEN THE SHORT PROGRAM AND THE LONG PROGRAM?

A bit of history will explain much. The Short Program was introduced shortly (get it?) after the 1972 Olympic Winter Games in Sapporo. The gold medal was won by Trixi Schuba of Austria, a superb skater of figures. Trixi was the best "figure" skater I have ever seen.

Her free skating was not superb.

She had received marks of first place for the Compulsory Figures and eighth place for the Free Skating.

(Eighth place was a gift.)

Despite this, Trixi was so respected and such a magnificent skater of figures that when she was called upon to take a bow after an exhibition, TV director Doug Wilson called to me to tell her that instead of doing a free skating encore, she should just skate a figure. She did. The audience gave her a standing ovation.

Karen Magnusson of Canada and Janet Lynn of the U.S. finished in second and third place respectively.

Janet had a reputation for not being able to do great figures. She was in seventh place after the figures. (As an aside, one of the judges later told her coach Slavka Kohout that a "block" of judges had kept her down in favor of the Austrian.)

It was not easy to control the judges and difficult to thoroughly educate them. It was not good for the Favorite Sport of the Olympic Winter Games that the winner of the gold medal was a great skater of figures, which were not televised and which few even showed up to watch, and an uninspiring free skater in the Free Skate competition, which everyone watched. So the powers that be then decided that the marking system itself had to be changed.

It was not the first time that a skater of very good figures who was less good in the Free Skate had won over first-rate free skaters. At the 1951 World Championships in Milan, Jeannette Altwegg of Switzerland won over Jacqueline du Bief (France), Tenley Albright and Sonja Klopfer (both from the U.S.), and Suzanne Morrow (Canada). All were outstanding free skaters.

During my time, the figures accounted for 60% of the total score, while the Free Skate had accounted for 40% of the total score. It was decided then that skaters would have to perform a Short Program that would account for 20% of the total score. The Free Skate remained at 40% of the total score. Thus figures at 40% of the total score were no longer in the majority.

Things did not remain that way for long. The figures were totally eliminated by 1990.

Then along came the pair skating scandal of the 2002 Olympic Winter Games in Salt Lake City (more on that in chapter 13). That debacle resulted in Ottavio Cinquanta, who was then and still is the President of the International Skating Union (ISU), creating a new International Judging System (IJS). The IJS was based on a very complicated marking system, the details of which I will bore you with in chapter 15.

(As an aside, the purpose of this new system was to try to solve the frequent judging disasters, such as cheating and "block judging," (multiple judges from different countries voting as a unit). Everything was to be based on points and little on subjectivity. The real purpose, however, was to make everything as secret (invisible) as possible and thus prevent the occurrence of another scandal like one in 2002 in Salt Lake City.)

So now a Short Program was instituted. How was it structured? How was it marked, and what was it supposed to prove?

It was to last two minutes. It was to be given two marks: one for its technical value and one for its artistic value.

Each skater was to perform seven specified required free skating elements, which were chosen each year. These elements (and thus the Short Program) were supposed to provide insight into the skaters' athletic and technical abilities. Skaters had to perform the prescribed spins, jumps, and other moves in a short piece of choreography to music of their own choice. While the Short Program required specific free skating moves, the Free Skate (Long Program) did not.

The 1972 Olympic gold medalist, Trixi Shuba, it was felt, was not sufficiently adept in free skating, and this new Short Program would reward free skaters and give free skating the majority of points available.

Today, the Short Program has gotten longer, and the Long Program (Free Skate) has gotten shorter. The moves in both are valued with points, and the two programs have grown similar because the same moves (particularly the highly valued ones) are usually done in both programs to gain as many points as possible.

Please take a look at some of the programs that were performed at the 2013 World Figure Skating Championships in London, Ontario. Then you will understand why there is basically no difference between the two programs of Patrick Chan, the Canadian champion and winner of the gold medal at these Championships, and those of Denis Ten of Kazakhstan, who won the silver medal.

In both the Short Program and the Long Program, both skaters start at or near center ice. Then both skaters in both (Short and Long) Programs do a few arm movements that try to set the scene but in a very minimal way. Then both skaters in both programs skate around the end of the rink, gaining speed. Then both skaters in both programs speed down the length of the rink and do either a triple Axel, a quadruple (quad) or a quad combination, or something of maximum difficulty. Then both skaters in both programs move toward their second high point-value jump, which is probably either a triple Axel, a quad, or a jump combination, depending on what the first jump was. Shortly after, they both do the first of three spins (the maximum allowed in both Short ad Long Programs), each of which has mostly the same positions in each program, although maybe in a different order. Then they both do step sequences and/or a choreographic sequence, and "linking movements" galore, along with minimal and very short selections of spirals and hippity hops, and a lot of "necessary" arm flailings.

The music in these skaters' Short and Long Programs (Free Skate) may be different, but the overall similarity between both programs is not the fault of the coach or the choreographer. In essence, both coach and choreographer must lay out the requirements before starting to choreograph the program and then hold the figure skating Rulebook in one hand and a computer in the other to access the clarifications and changes that are issued weekly by the Technical Committee of the ISU (coming out on Thursday and going into effect the following Monday). Then they can start being the bean counters they have had to become.

It is not a comfortable state in which to create.

You may be saying, "All right already, Mr. Know-It-All. It's easy to criticize, but much harder to create. How would *you* do it?"

That question puts me on the spot!

The only way I can answer is to tell you what I did when I had the opportunity to create a competition. For me, it was like painting on a blank canvas. And I painted it the best I could for that event and at that time.

The event was the World Professional Figure Skating Championship.

The opportunity first came about in 1972. At many Olympic Games, one or more athletes become the story, the darlings, of the press and of the Games. Janet Lynn was the darling of the 1972 Olympic Winter Games in Sapporo. Her small size, her blond hair, and her smile made her a favorite of the Japanese.

Everyone there wanted another chance to see her. So we created the World Professional Figure Skating Championship. It was held in Tokyo in 1973.
I invited men, ladies, and pair skaters to come. The men's event included Ronnie Robertson, Don Jackson, Don Knight, and John Misha Petkevich. The pair skating event included Ludmila Belousova and Oleg Protopopov, Almut Lehmann and Herbert Wiesinger, Cynthia and Ronald Kaufman, and Susan Behrens and Richard Dwyer. Janet Lynn competed in the ladies' competition, along with Cathy Lee Irwin and Zsuzsa Almassy.

When we created the 1973 World Professional Figure Skating Championship, the format and event were not complicated.

First, I had to create the rules. Although I had understood the rules of skating competitions for some forty years, I knew little about creating rules that would work for this event. I did know that in this situation, as in most, less was more.

So certain rules were immediately shaped:

1.   There would be two programs.
The first would be technically oriented, and the second would emphasize the creative side of skating. These two

views were the descendants of the two marks traditionally given for free skating in "amateur" competitions: "Technical Merit" and "Artistic Impression."

2. There were to be no time limits.

Then and still today, I feel that the skaters themselves (along with their choreographers and coaches) should be the judges of what they can do best. The programs of my day were five minutes long. That length of time could be difficult for a program that required both technical moves and a high performance level (particularly in a high-altitude venue).

When it comes to music, time limits can force skaters and their choreographers to slaughter the composer's intentions. The restrictive time limits still in place are, in my humble opinion, absurd. I know full well the television networks need to know the duration of each program, but all they have to do is ask!

Also, there is a feeling on the part of sports folks that everyone should be given the same time limits. But why? Is this a race?

To jam a piece of music into an arbitrary time limit is like saying, "Dear Mr. Tchaikovsky: Would you mind shortening that final crescendo, because it's too long to fit my program? And while you're at it, could you please put a "bop" at the end, because that supports the arm movement that I'm doing to signify the end of the program?"

The event was not repeated until the December following the 1980 Olympic Winter Games in Lake Placid. But in 1980, different conditions existed. The purpose remained the same, and that was to prove who was the best skater among all skaters, both amateur and professional. Remember, it was common for skaters who had reached a peak medaling at national or world championships or at the Olympic Games to retire to earn a living. So the pick of the crop of the very best skaters was available.

The same question of "who is the best?" had faced us when we created a new TV program (also in 1973) called *The Superstars*, which set out to prove who was the best athlete in the world. This question had been on my mind since 1949. In 1949, I won the James Sullivan Award as America's Outstanding Amateur Athlete. The year before, I had won the 1948 Olympic gold medal for figure skating. As wonderful as these accolades were, what niggled at me was the fact that of the twelve boys in my class at the Englewood School for Boys, ten were better athletes than I was. Yet I got the Sullivan Award as America's best amateur athlete—me, who as a kid was so bad at baseball that the outfield would sit down when I stepped up to bat. Then about twelve years after I received the Sullivan Award, *Life* magazine published a full-page photo of Edward Villella, a principal dancer with George Balanchine's New York City Ballet. Villella was a boxer in the Marine Corps but had always wanted to dance. The photo showed Eddie in a startling jump that in skating terminology would be called a stag jump. The headline above the photo read: "Is This America's Best Athlete?" There was that same question again!

The Superstars was designed to pit top athletes from a variety of sports against each other in many sports (but not in the one they were famous for). The sports included tennis, swimming, track, weight lifting, biking, and an obstacle race.

We got the best of the best athletes possible.

The first edition in 1973 included pole vaulter Bob Seagren, skier Jean-Claude Killy, football player Johnny Unitas, tennis player Rod Laver, race car driver Peter Revson, baseball player Johnny Bench, basketball player Elvin Hayes, hockey player Rod Gilbert, bowler Jim Stefanich, and boxer Joe Frazier. They were all the best in their fields. It was not necessary to convince them that this event would be serious competition. At first some thought it would be a lark, but then the endorphins and competitive juices started flowing, and when you saw Pete Rose fighting for every tennis point, you knew they took it seriously. Some athletes like O.J. Simpson came thinking they could win it easily, and when they didn't, they went back, trained for it, returned and won. The competitive spirit was foremost.

However, for the World Professional Figure Skating Championship in 1980, it was necessary to convince the top skaters to participate. Some of them had performed in shows but had not competed for some time. For most athletes, competition is continuously the name of the game until they retire. But remember when skaters thought of competition, they thought of the National Championships, the World Championships, or the Olympic Games. When they retired from competition, they were able to earn excellent livings from exhibition (show) skating, not competitive skating. The biggest concern expressed was, "I might lose my Olympic title!" It was difficult to change the mindset of skaters like Peggy Fleming and Dorothy Hamill that they could never "lose" their Olympic title. "Once an Olympian, always an Olympian" was and is a motto of the International Olympic Committee!

John Curry understood the situation instantly, quickly commenting, "I understand what you are doing. You are creating a skating show, but with the extra added value that someone will win."

I realized, however, that it would be necessary not to embarrass the skaters by emphasizing who won rather than cheering all. So for the first four years of the show, I created it as a team competition. The skaters were divided into red and blue teams, and not only did each skater have to do two programs, but each team had to perform a group number, all of which counted toward the total score of each team.

I also made sure there would be no three-tiered awards platform with one skater standing higher than another.

It worked. The 1980 World Pro (as it came to be known) included Peggy Fleming, Dorothy Hamill, Linda Fratianne, and Emi Watanabe. The pair skaters were Tai Babilonia and Randy Gardner, and JoJo Starbuck and Ken Shelley. The ice dancers were Jim Millns and Colleen O'Connor, and Krisztina Regöczy and András Sallay. The men were John Curry, Robin Cousins, Charlie Ticknor, and Gordon McKellen. It was a dazzling group of great skaters.

I made sure the arena owners would guarantee that the first 15 rows would be filled so no empty seats would be seen on camera. It turned out I did not need to worry about that. The arena was in Landover, a one-hour ride outside Washington, D.C. It was filled. In fact, the seats were always filled throughout the almost thirty-year run of the World Pro (quite unlike many of today's events where the seats often remain half empty).

As an aside, "Landover," as it was sometimes called, was the most perfect arena for audience viewing. The seats rose in a single continuous climb up to the top, on a sharp curve so no one seemed to be far from the action. There were no corporate boxes to interrupt the flow or the view. It was a less profitable design, and eventually Landover went the way of the dustbin. But I have never seen a more pleasant and audience-friendly arena.

I also knew it would take a four-year Olympic cycle for skaters to become accustomed to seeing professionals compete. Then I would not need to use the team concept, but could revert to my original head-to-head concept. By 1984, everyone was used to and looked forward to the event and to taking part in it. It became a highlight of the skating year.

The success of this event, like the success of all events on television, was quickly copied. We established the Challenge of Champions for ABC and assorted other events. Promoters attempted to copy the format. They were less successful.

It was important to arrive at a straightforward yet fair set of rules for the event.

1. I again called for two programs, one of which emphasized athleticism and the other emphasizing artistry.

Oleg Protopopov constantly reminded me, saying, "Deek! Deek! You cannot have technical merit without artistry, but neither can you have artistry without technical merit." That was and remained the defining formula for the World Professional Figure Skating Championships, which as mentioned ran for some thirty years and was one of the most successful skating events in the history of skating.

1. In the first program, the technical mark accounted for 60% of the total score, while the artistic impression mark was 40% of the total. In the second program, the technical value counted for 40% and the artistic impression mark counted for 60% of the total. Both programs thus contained evaluations for both artistry and technical merit, but in different proportions.

2. There was also to be no time limit.

However, I like to paraphrase the song from *My Fair Lady* and say, "I'm an ordinary man who desires nothing more than an ordinary chance to live exactly as I like." And being an ordinary fellow, I would, if pushed, support a technical program having a time limit (as long as it was a generous one). This is to show that I am indeed a "reasonable" man who would certainly not filibuster a government shutdown over the identity of Short and Long programs.

At one point after the World Pro had been running for a while, I counted the time lengths of every program skated and found that only once did someone skate less than three minutes and only twice did someone skate longer than five minutes. So just to make sure no one skated a program reenacting "The Rise and Fall of the

Roman Empire," which would last into the middle of next week, I suggested that time lengths should be not less than three minutes nor more than five-and-a-half minutes. However, there was to be no penalty if they did exceed the limit. No one did!

1. The marks were to be based on a perfect score of 10 to distinguish this event from amateur competitions (those were the days when things were still "amateur" or "professional"). That distinction was eliminated twenty years later because of the success of the World Pro. (Now, *that* was a compliment!)

It seems the ISU did not like someone else (me) organizing "championships" which they considered to be their preserve. So they extinguished the distinction of amateur/professional and started paying the skaters to skate in National and World events providing, they did not appear in any "non-official event" (meaning one they had not sanctioned—meaning any competition that I produced!).

So I am honored to say, "You are welcome" to those skaters who either had their careers at least partially revived after being off prime time sports television or to those amateurs who then were and are now being paid!

Oh, well! A good deed never goes unnoticed (by me, at least)!

1. There were to be no restrictions on costumes. That opened the way for some pretty inventive ideas. One skater appeared with only one skate, while wearing on the other foot only a red sock. She was not rewarded much for that program.

2. We constantly reminded the skaters and the judges: "You can't have artistry without technique, but neither can you have technique without artistry." The judges were instructed that a truly great spiral could be as difficult to do as yet another triple jump. Now, that may seem like a

foolish mandate, particularly in today's terms, but remember how many spirals we all have seen that are memorably forgettable.

And then there are some that are unforgettable. Michelle Kwan's spiral covered the whole rink, changing from an inside edge to an outside edge in a huge serpentine, and was skated with a winning smile that had the audience clapping as they saw it coming. It was and should be marked with a very high performance value. Sasha Cohen's spiral had extraordinary leg elevation, a superb back position, and a glorious overall quality. Clearly both Kwan's and Cohen's spirals were memorable and should probably come close to being equal in value, but for different reasons. Cohen's had high "technical merit" value, while Kwan's had high "performance" (artistic impression) value.

1. All the judges who were asked to participate had impeccable reputations and had been champions of note or had built great reputations in one aspect or another of figure skating. No one represented a country. Only once or twice did a judge fail to live up to the obligation. They were not invited back.

But keep in mind that even the best judges are only human. This led some of them at one point to so relish the applause they received when they rewarded a skater who was an audience favorite with a perfect score of 10 that they started feeling insecure and began giving 10s willy-nilly. Like many judges over the years, they did not like to be booed for giving a low mark to a popular skater who was having a bad day.

As an irrelevant but informative slant on judging in the world of "amateur" skating, one of the most virulent displays of public bias occurred in the 1960s. At that time Dr. Suzanne Morrow Francis, who had competed in singles, pair, and dance events, was Canadian and North American Champion, as well as a World and Olympic competitor, had become a judge. She wore a bright red coat when she judged. In the 1964 Olympic Winter Games in Innsbruck, she placed Ludmila Belousova and Oleg Protopopov first in the pair skating competition. But she had also elevated Canadian skaters Debbi Wilkes and Guy Revell over Marika Kilius and Hans-Jürgen Bäumler of West Germany. Whether that was justified or not, she was the only judge who had voted that way. When she appeared on a street in her red coat where a large contingent of West Germans (who were Kilius-Bäumler fans) had come to see the competitions, she was dubbed the "Red Devil," spat on, booed, and pushed off the curb.

The ISU, whether rightly or wrongly, suspended her for bias. But the physical abuse was above and beyond what anyone should have to endure and is never appropriate.

The multiple awards of 10s at the World Pro kept me from being a happy camper. I quickly scheduled a judges meeting and made sure that one and all understood that they had to respect the judging framework, and that anyone who gave a 10 had to be able to explain in detail why it was a perfect program and compare it to all others. The 10s stopped. Sanity returned. My belief was that the judges were to be respected as intelligent human beings, and even if they needed guidance and parameters, they were to be allowed to judge as they saw best.

I was very proud of their overall record.

13 IT'S CALLED FIGURE SKATING, BUT THERE AIN'T ANY FIGURES

OK, dear couch companions, it is called figure skating . . . but there aren't any figures in it! Go figure!

Of course, it is only in English-speaking countries that the Fine Art of Figure Skating is called Figure Skating. Other countries call it *patinage artistique*, or *Eiskunstlauf* or *pattinaggio artistico su ghiaccio*.

This prompts the question: where are we? And how did we get here?

I have often felt that if we don't know where we have been, it may be hard to know where we are going or if we are "there" yet—or for that matter, where "there" even is. In the sixteenth, seventeenth, and eighteenth centuries, folks took up skating with enthusiasm. For centuries it had been a means of transportation during winter and also a source of fun and pleasure.

It was recorded in paintings by Hendrick Avercamp, the Bruegels, Gilbert Stuart, Winslow Homer, Henry Raeburn, Eastman Johnson and Toulouse Lautrec. During the "Frost Fairs" on the Thames at times when the river froze solid between the 1600s and the early 1800s, the whole city of London—skaters, carriages, food vendors, barbers, and all sorts of ordinary and not so ordinary folks—moved onto the ice.

Soon, fancy moves that made tracings on the ice began to be developed by gentlemen, including cross cuts, a Maltese cross, moves with rockers, three turns and brackets, running grapevines, and even writing your name in the ice. For many years, figure skating was called 'Fancy Skating."

In 1782, the American artist Gilbert Stuart painted a portrait of one William Grant skating in Hyde Park in London. Elegant, with arms crossed, he was pictured skating a left forward outside edge. The portrait is eight feet tall, an iconic fixture of the National Gallery in Washington, and the painting that made Gilbert Stuart's name.

It was at one time lent to the Metropolitan Museum of Art for an exhibition of Stuart's work. A group of us interested in American arts called The William Cullen Bryant Fellows of the American Wing toured the exhibition and listened to the curators who were providing commentary. I asked if anyone knew what the very small skaters in the distance in the middle of the painting were doing. No one knew.

I did. It was my one and only contribution to Art History.

The small figures depicted gentlemen skating toward each other on a serpentine-shaped lake (which was called The Serpentine—duh!) Like gentlemen, they would greet each other. It was the equivalent of two knights in armor lifting their visors to show they were friendly and not the enemy, or like gentlemen today taking their hats off in greeting a lady.

The difference here was that they were skating. On seeing each other, they each skated a forward outside edge to their right, changing to an inside edge and going from that forward inside edge on one foot to a back inside edge on the other foot while simultaneously doffing their hats.

They were actually doing what is today called a "Mohawk." To be honest, I don't know why it was called a Mohawk except the Mohawk Indians were around and on coins and every other kind of insignia. (As an aside, there's another step move called a "Choctaw," so maybe now we are getting closer to something!)

This change from front to back explains their bent knee positions as they doff their hats. They then skate off on a back outside edge on the other foot.

Thus each of the skaters was skating a serpentine on a lake called The Serpentine, and this move became known as the Serpentine Greeting. In other cities and other countries, gentlemen created their own "greetings." In Philadelphia there was both a Philadelphia Greeting and a Pennsylvania Greeting.

I hope someday you will have the chance to come by my garden and see an "Homage to Figures" that I created in a circular space. The gates are designed in three panels. The center contains both left and right foot loops and crosscuts (designs that were in many of the "old figures" of skating), while the outside panels depict a "Single" and a "Double" greeting!

Small pleasures enjoyed by small minds!

The middle of the nineteenth century saw the beginning of skating performances when skaters like William H. Fuller, Jackson Haines, and Callie Curtis began to give exhibitions in the U.S., Europe, and even the Far East.

In England, Queen Victoria skated with Prince Albert. She had the most intriguing and elaborate pair of skates, with the front of the blades cut into swan shapes. There were engravings down the length of the blade. In Vienna, Emperor Franz Joseph II skated to the music of Johann Strauss.

Competitions began, too. William H. Fuller of Boston won the Championship of America in 1865, and when he went to Europe, a poster circa 1867 advertised his appearance without a name, printing only: "*Allez Voir Le Grand Patineur.*" That poster now hangs in my kitchen.

In the 1870s, social distinctions began to develop with the founding in 1888 of the National Amateur Skating Association. Professionals who were paid for exhibitions were further distinguished from amateurs who weren't paid.

Then the first of the modern Olympics were revived in 1896, and skating was included in the London Games in 1908.

Only men entered the events. Ulrich Salchow of Sweden won ten World titles between 1901 and 1911 and was the first to do a "Salchow" (now we understand what a Salchow is—and it's not a sick cow!). Then in 1902, Madge Syers, an Englishwoman, entered the event and placed second behind Salchow.

Separate competitions for men and ladies were soon established!

(It figures, and a cry of "Good grief!" might not be inappropriate here.)

Professional shows became more elaborate, featuring stars in the 1920s like Charlotte (whose last name was Oelschlagel, but as previously mentioned she went by her first name. sort of like Cher, Oprah, and Madonna do today). Then Sonja Henie, famous from her Olympic triumphs, made movies and appeared in shows like the Hollywood Ice Revue, along with Ice Capades, Ice Follies, and Holiday on Ice, which attracted millions of viewers. During all this time, skating became more structured, with different associations being started, including the International Skating Union (ISU) in 1892. The ISU controlled both figure skating and speed skating.

And the rules of competition became more structured. "Imagination," inherent in the skating of wonderful designs like folk art drawings, all but disappeared when the ice melted.

Before World War II, singles skaters had to skate six

figures starting on each foot, for a total of twelve figures. Following the War, and for the first time, the 1947 World Championships required only six figures starting on either the right or the left foot, depending on a random draw. These figures were all prescribed in the Rulebook, and there were forty-one of them. They were based on the two-lobed figure eight (two circles). Three-lobed figures were called serpentines (there's that name again) or a "change of edge figure," and there were also rockers and counters. There was a "one-foot figure" (where the entire figure eight was skated on one foot), and some with turns like three turns, double threes and brackets. All were precisely codified in the Rulebook.

They were called "Compulsory Figures," and this part of the competition took as long as two days. (Remember, it was called *figure skating*.)

The figures counted for 60% of the total score.

Mamma mia! That was a lot of figures and a lot of scores!

Come to think of it, there should have been a second gold medal just for the Compulsory Figures in those days. Actually, later on, there was—but it soon disappeared when figures declined in importance, quality, and general popularity, and were eventually eliminated!

Both in form and function, "Compulsory Figures" were even more different from the "free skating" portion of the competition than a mile run is from a hundred-yard dash. It also became clear that knowing how to do figures was not necessary in order to become a first-class free skater, that learning them took up enormous amounts of practice and competition time, and that doing figures could work against keeping the body limber and truly stretched. They were not the equivalent of practicing at the barre for dancers, stretching exercises for athletes, or scales at a piano for pianists.

However, they had great importance as a means of teaching edges, turns, control, balance, focus, body positions and changes of positions, and what a "lean of the body" truly meant.

When they were original creations made up by the skaters out of their imaginations, they were an art form in themselves, like the intricate penmanship drawings of the nineteenth century.

I recently was part of a television show in Canada called *Battle of the Blades*. It paired a hockey player and a figure skater against other similar pairs. It was clear from the beginning that the hockey stars did not understand what it meant to "check" (i.e., stop the rotation of) the shoulders (as opposed to body checks) or how to use leg and arm positions to control an edge, or what a lean of the body was, and how to turn from forward to backward or vice versa without having to jump from two feet onto two feet.

As they learned about the Fine Art of Figure Skating, every one of the hockey greats who participated said they would have been better hockey players if they had taken up figure skating. Every one said they would insist that their hockey-playing sons take up figure skating in order to improve their turning control and quickness of movement.

There was one particular performance during this TV series that illustrated these differences. It was a side-by-side pair performance by World Champion skaters Kurt Browning and Barbara Underhill that was one of the finest skating moments I have seen. Both skaters wore hockey skates (no toe picks, narrower blades, less depth in the curve between the blade edges). Yet both were able to highlight and emphasize the extraordinary flow of figure skating at its best—the deep edges, the precise turns, the smooth backward and forward movements—with the greatest stylish position.

It was an invigorating experience.

When I was twenty-two, I had the nerve to write an autobiography. I must have thought I knew what life was all about. (Wrong! I still don't have a clue!)

But I did feel that figures, while important, were not *more* important than free skating, and that lowering the figures from 60% of the total score to 50% should be considered. I thought I was being calm, cool, collected, and truly sophisticated by treating the subject so gingerly and not being a radical, urging massive reduction of the importance of figures. Little did I know that, as the century moved forward, they would be reduced, then further reduced, and finally eliminated altogether, due to the vision of one ISU official: Sonia Bianchetti.

And to think it only took half a century!

The art of skating figures, a true expression of folk art, has unfortunately been lost to the history books. Although some figures are still done, the elaborate, magical concoctions of the nineteenth century mostly disappeared when the ice melted. The figures that are included in the step sequences or choreographic sequences in today's skating rules are limited in elegance and quality and are mere pastiches of the original figures.

It was inevitable that figures would disappear. Yet it is also inevitable that the values they taught will also disappear. Arguments for getting rid of them and for keeping them exist. Maybe a simple solution could be arranged that would allow both a presence but not a dominance. (Dream on, Dickie Boy!)

Has this long discussion left us with empty glasses and scraping the bottom of the guacamole bowl? Well, go get a refill of both, 'cause you haven't talked skating 'til you've talked scoring.

Before the scoring scandal at the 2002 Olympic Winter Games in Salt Lake City, a perfect score or mark in figure skating was 6.0.

Pop quiz! Does anyone remember why the perfect mark was a 6?

While the first purpose of skating was practical—transportation—the second was expressive: the ability to do fancy skating (including "figures") was the hallmark of a gentleman's accomplishment in the sport.

When a figure eight was skated, it was done three times on each foot: first one circle on the right foot, then one circle on the left foot. Then this sequence was repeated twice more. Three circles on the right foot plus three circles on the left foot equal six circles. Even for a one-foot figure, there would be six total tracings to count and judge.

Voilà! The score of 6 was created. While certainly not as dramatic as a Bo Derek "10" (if you don't know Bo Derek, watch the movie *10!*), still a 6 became an icon of the sport, and everyone wanted a 6. I even got one in the 1948 Olympic Games. Ice dancers Torvill and Dean got 14,000.

The public learned to recognize the meaning of a 6 in skating. It was a score that we on the couch felt we could debate, complain about, and disagree about among ourselves. It made us feel we could understand something of what it took to excel at the Fine Art of Figure Skating. It gave us a feeling of being on the "inside."

All during this time, the judging was totally subjective, but like all subjective judging, it was easily challengeable (corrupted?). And subjective judging led to "peculiar" judging (crooked judging?).

The stories of crooked judging in Sonja Henie's day and all through the twentieth century were numerous and well known. When the 1927 World Championship was held in Oslo, Norway, the skater Herma Szabo, the defending champion, reported that the city of Oslo was plastered with posters of Sonja (paid for by her father) and the seven judges consisted of one Austrian judge, one German judge, and three Norwegian judges. It was a shoo-in for Sonja.

Also rampant were outright payments of cash or goods and "block" judging: judges from several countries agreeing on how they would judge ("you vote for mine; I'll vote for yours"). The United States, Canada, and Japan were mostly out of the block judging scene. The Americans had a tradition of individualism. Canada was wildly independent and wouldn't listen to anything Americans requested anyway, and Japan was too far away and the language barrier made it difficult. This distance of geography also applies to the British (and maybe the language, too, considering the first-rate edging of the English accent!).

I don't hold credence that block judging would not have been possible had the United States been made up of individual countries—per the original plan. Thus a "Block" of New York, New Jersey, and Pennsylvania versus Vermont and New Hampshire would have been easy.

I firmly believe that many judges (not only the Americans) did yeoman service that was honest. The Soviet juggernaut and some of the neighboring European countries were far more ruthless, politically experienced, and accustomed to intrigue. The close proximity of countries that had been politically intertwined for centuries was far more lethal than what the U.S., Canada, and Japan could muster.

In skating, there was no security in trying to win by a fraction of a point. It was unlike a horse race, where one could win "by a nose," or a track race, where a "split second" win was legitimate. One had to win by being at least 25% better than the nearest opponent.

It was a dicey world!

And, like most dishonest things, it eventually erupted.

It was that dishonesty that culminated in the startling events that occurred in 1999 and again in the 2002 Olympic Winter Games in Salt Lake City—events that finally signaled publicly the problems, if not the threat to the very health and life, of the Fine Art of Figure Skating.

In the 1999 World Championships in Helsinki, Canadian TV caught on camera two judges, Yuri Babenko of Russia and Alfred Korytek of the Ukraine, signaling to each other, by tapping their feet with the placement

175

numbers they would give. I quickly referred to them as the "tap-dancing judges."

Both were suspended by the ISU. Both suspensions were short (one and two years). Both suspensions were later reduced. Both judges were back judging in no time at all.

Hello!!!

Another factor was the tradition of judges who lived in one country judging for another country. Judges who lived in Moscow frequently judged for other smaller countries (like Belarus) that might not have had any creditable judges but needed to keep their Federations alive. This also allowed the mother country (Russia) to control more votes.

Three years later, at the 2002 Olympic Winter Games in Salt Lake City, the "Scandal of Salt Lake City" occurred. As most of you on the couch (if you're not asleep by now) will remember, the French judge, Madame Marie-Reine Le Gougne, confessed to being forced (by threat of elimination of further judging opportunities) by the president of the French Federation, Didier Gailhaguet, himself a former figure skater, to put the Russian pair skaters Elena Berezhnaya and Anton Sikharulidze first in the pair skating event over Jamie Salé and David Pelletier of Canada. In return, the Russian judge would put the French ice dancers Marina Anissina and Gwendal Peizerat first in the ice dance event.

The closeness of the pair skating competition between Canada and Russia was extreme. Le Gougne burst into tears, confessing the pressure on her. Thus was brought to light one of the worst moments of crooked dealings and dishonor in sports history.

The press was ablaze with worldwide continuous reporting of the event. The president of the International Olympic Committee (IOC), Jacques Rogge, must have been appalled at the never-ending coverage of the pair skating scandal and anxious that the press talk about something else for the second week of the Olympic Games.

Remember, the International Olympic Committee (IOC) controls the operation of the Olympic Games and delegates control of each sport to the International Federation (IFS). In figure skating, the IFS is the International Skating Union (ISU).

(If this is already confusing, then make a small chart, or just forget it and have some nuts, of which there are plenty around!)

At this time, the head of the ISU was an Italian by the name of Ottavio Cinquanta (in order to save paper and thus trees and help the greening of the world, we have decided to sometimes refer to him as "OC").

The ISU governs two sports, speed skating and figure skating. Speed skaters and figure skaters have sometimes alternated as president, depending on who was the most popular and worked the political scene the best.
However, there has been no figure skater president in more than 40 years.

Remember the current president of the ISU is Ottavio Cinquanta. Mr. Cinquanta is a speed skater.

I would like to dedicate this chapter (but not the whole book) to Mr. Cinquanta for his

HONESTY!!!
in stating repeatedly,
"I am a speed skater. I know nothing about figure skating."
If you think I am being snarky, read the next chapter to find out why.

14 IT'S DA RULES, BABY

So now we have a full-blown scandal on our hands!

Jacques Rogge, President of the IOC (the International Olympic Committee), must have spoken! The problem was to be fixed, and fixed *now*! And it was in Ottavio Cinquanta's lap.

I have often said that if you know what a man wants, you will know what his agenda will be. Ottavio Cinquanta (remember, we sometimes call him OC) was a member of the IOC, but only because he was the president of the ISU. When he retired as president of the ISU (and that's another story, believe me!), he would no longer be a member of the IOC. On the other hand, if anyone becomes a permanent member of the IOC, that individual would receive very generous perks for life. That's a carrot worth reaching for.

It is always difficult to get a committee together *now*! But the pressure here was tremendous. The powers that be met and the decision was instantly made to split the gold and give two gold medals, one each to both the Canadian and Russian pair skaters. But this splitting was nothing more than a temporary Band-Aid. It succeeded in shutting up the press, at least to some degree.

The real problem was how to quiet down the judging crisis and remove the chances of another scandal? And so, OC called for the creation of a new International Judging System (IJS).

(At this point there are so many initials floating around here, you might think I've poured alphabet soup in our beer!)

So OC set out to put in place this new system, the IJS. He had already been the president for over a decade. The scandal finally forced him to act. Was that a case of thinking ahead?

The system had to be foolproof. It was supposed to correct the age-old tradition of block judging, of nationalism, of the trading of votes, the receiving of gifts, and the buying of points.

My, oh my! This was a complicated world.

Some countries needed the skaters to get high rankings to get their government's financial support (no money if they did not have a skater who qualified for the Olympics). Some countries needed to get money from the ISU from television income for their own sport's operations. Some individuals just wanted income to pay for their own support.

Figure skating had considerably more income than speed skating. Guess which organization provided the support for the other organization? Guess which sport OC came from?

So a new system was worked out. There was to be no more subjective judging. Everything was to have points awarded. (We'll get another beer and talk about the new system in the next chapter.)

But the real goal was something else, and it was the most insidious element possible.

Everything was to be hidden from public scrutiny!

No longer would the press or anyone, including you and me, be able to uncover a scandal. No longer would anyone know what score a particular judge had awarded.

No longer would anyone know which judge's score had been counted, which also meant there was no way to know how each country had voted.

Secrecy was the color, the flavor, the substance of the new system. That was the real goal.

A task force was established to develop a new judging system. It was a task force that was made up of computer guys and eventually moved to a German company to work out the issues. The new judging system cost a fortune and is still being added to.

It would be a complicated system. But remember, it must have been necessary to get it fixed NOW! Sometimes one can bury a lot of sins in the mode of urgency. Get it done now! Hurry! Hurry! "No questions."

And it was here that OC's extraordinary ability for manipulation came into play.

1. He presented the IJS (the International Judging System) to the ISU Congress ONGRESS in 2003. He presented it to the Congress as a "project." If it had been presented as a "rule," it would have been sent to the Figure Skating section of the Congress that would then have considered it.

2. The important point is that by presenting it as a "project," it could be voted on by both speed and figure skaters. So he repeatedly (forty-one times) called it a "project," not a rule, and also repeatedly said it was a "journey" that everyone was taking to determine a new system.

3. Ottavio Cinquanta (who is called "Il Duce" by the very prominent newspaperwoman Christine Brennan), knowing that it would be delayed by the time needed to consider it, instantly dismissed any questions about the IJS.

4. The IJS was then voted on and was passed as a "project" by both speed skaters and figure skaters.

5. When it appeared in the Rulebook, it was labeled a "Rule."

(Another aside! Remember, this was a journey to develop a new judging system for figure skating. But it was being led by a speed skater who had often stated, "I am a speed skater. I know nothing about figure skating.")

And guess what? Was the Congress controlled by OC? Or did the delegates want to please OC in order to receive continued support for themselves and/or their Federations? Did the number of delegates who were speed skaters like OC tip the balance? Most speed skaters didn't know or care what went on in the figure skating world. Of course, the new IJS was voted in.

It was major disinformation that OC fed to the world of figure skating.

I am sure President Obama would wish for similar talents when facing the battle between the Republicans and the Democrats.

(If this talk about politics hasn't put you to sleep, I can always tell you some jokes.)

So the International Judging System (IJS) was established.

If one runs for and becomes president of an organization, one should know what the organization he is president of does. It is not sufficient merely to say, "I know nothing about it." Learn it or at least respect those who do understand it. Ottavio Cinquanta violated the meaning of being a president.

Don't despair. I will give you a *short* description of this system in the next chapter, leaving us plenty of relaxing time to settle back and watch the advertisements and sneak in a swig of hooch from the bottle under the couch.

15 THE INTERNATIONAL JUDGING SYSTEM (IJS)

First, don't shoot me if I say that while the old judging system was flawed, it was also reparable.

I have repeatedly said both in commentary and elsewhere that the overall results were many times in the right order if, and only if, it was perceived that there was a large enough gap between one skater and the others in the overall quality of their performance. Examples are ice dancers Torvill and Dean and ladies singles figure skater Dorothy Hamill, who outdistanced the field. There are others, too, but the perceived gap was not so universal. Skaters like Robin Cousins and John Curry who should and did win were nevertheless subject to some fancy figuring.

This is my personal opinion, so don't take away my beer.

Others won fairly and correctly under the previous judging system. Still others won when the conflict was clearly between two skaters who were perceived to be best, but who also came from the same country. The operative words here are "from the same country," so little national

183

bias could get into play. Note that in the 2002 Olympic Winter Games in Salt Lake City, the two top skaters in the men's event were Alexei Yagudin and Evgeni Plushenko, both of whom were Russian.

But clearly it was an imperfect system.

There were several problems.

Neither judges nor countries were penalized severely enough for transgressions.

If you are a skating judge convicted multiple times of cheating, or if your country (Federation) is convicted of multiple offenses, you should both be *out*!

This clearly was not possible when the Federations themselves were in charge   (i.e., when the fox was in charge of the hen house?), but it could have been applied much more severely to many more judges and Federations. Before anyone starts throwing eggs at me, take a quick look at the record. Between 1970 and 1977, thirteen judges from the Soviet Union were given year-long suspensions. Then in 1977 the Soviet Union (which at that time, incidentally, had the ability to control and did control many other countries and their Federations included in what was known as the "Eastern Bloc," such as Bulgaria, Czechoslovakia, East Germany, Hungary, Poland, Rumania, et cetera) was suspended and for one year (1978) was not allowed to send any judges to any ISU event. One year was clearly not long enough, but then small gifts are always appreciated.

Even if it was too little, it was the way to control errant folks and Federations.   (We won't talk about the howl that went up.)

It was also well known that many judges were honest but were totally under the thumb of their Federation, which could many times be under the thumb of their government and had to bow when asked to bow.

The plot thimkens! (That's correctly spelled in a world as off-kilter as this one). So the new judging system (IJS) went into place. The problem with this is that it is a system that is a speed skater's vision. Everything must be timed or measured. It's all about who can do the most turns in the air, use the most arm, leg, edge, and body positions.

Then give them all points.

Then remove from the judges any significant ability to judge.

Under the new system, skaters first receive marks for Technical Scores. Grab a handful of popcorn (well, maybe two) and listen to what that entails.

First, there is a *base value* assigned to every element, i.e., every spin, jump, and step sequence. Other moves include a multitude of other twinky things like Twizzles, toe popping, bends at the waist, and flailing arms.

There are *levels of difficulty*. For example, a spin with one change of foot but no change of position (i.e., an upright spin that doesn't change to a sit spin) has levels of difficulty going from Basic Level to Level 4, which has point increases from 1.7 to 3.2, depending on the particular spin chosen.

Then there is the *grade of execution (GOE)*. The judges must assign a grade to each move of +1, +2, +3, or -1, -2, or -3. There is also a zero (0) if you are not thinking and have let your mind wander and think it is neither good nor bad. (My goodness!)

Then there is a Technical Panel comprised of three people: a Technical Controller, a Technical Specialist, and an Assistant Technical Specialist, plus a Replay Operator and a Data Operator. The Replay Operator video records the elements, and the Data Operator enters them into the computer system. The Assistant Technical Specialist helps the Technical Specialist identify the elements skated and the level of difficulty of each element (these folks often include skaters of national or international repute or coaches). Their decisions are supervised by the Technical Controller.

By the way, in case you forgot, there is also a Judges

panel and a Referee!

(I have to repeat these facts often; otherwise, I would lose track!)

The entire set of Technical Rules is complicated, and every coach or choreographer knows that the emphasis is on following the rules and that in order to do this, he or she needs to become a bean counter!

One further point is that new "Changes, Clarifications and Amendments" to rules are published on the ISU Web site on Thursday and go into effect the following Monday. So God help you if your pupil is competing shortly thereafter and you miss something!

All of this makes two things necessary. One, as I've mentioned before, is that the choreographer or coach must have a computer in one hand and the figure skating Rulebook in the other in order to create (repeat: *create!*) a work of substance. If you don't think this is correct, ask any coach or choreographer who is not a Technical Specialist or Technical Controller, as the latter have their travel, lodging, food, and a small daily allowance paid for by the ISU for the services they provide at international championships. They won't get rich on this support, but if they enjoy attending events, as most do, all their expenses are paid. So they won't look a gift horse in the mouth.

It is discouraging, to say the least.

Now, to those of you who have not gone off to snooze in never-never land, I want you to know that the creative side of the sport is intended to be covered by the Program Component Scores, with the results listed and announced on TV by the commentators right after the Technical Scores. These are marks given for what used to be called Artistic Impression, which referred to the theatrical, creative, musical, performance, and "artistic" aspects of a program.

These Program Component Scores are listed as (please, don't hold your breath) the following:

1.   Skating Skills

2. Transitions/Linking Footwork and Movement
3. Performance/Execution
4. Composition/Choreography
5. Interpretation/Timing

Each of these components includes anywhere from three to seven criteria, together totaling 26.

For your own amusement, try to take on the judging role and value these 26 criteria over five components in the few seconds you have to think about it (i.e., after the performance is over and before you have to give the mark.)

Try again. Then try yet again. Only then are you justified in throwing the bowl of guacamole at me.

But please, please, please, will someone on the couch explain the REAL differences here? For example, isn't choreography footwork? There must be a cutoff when a transition ends and a linking movement starts, and what determines that exact second?

Composition/Choreography and Transitions/Linking Footwork and Movement are all overlapping and similar and really cause a headache trying to decipher what is what. The phrase "Linking Movements" sounded marvelous when uttered in a high voice on TV by an English lady friend who was famed for her work with T and D. But that was years ago, before there was an IJS.

OK, guys, I know that there are elaborate criteria for each of the Program Component Scores, and I understand the reasons for concern. So, folks sitting on this now-lumpy couch with me, do you remember when skaters led up to a difficult jump with a very long approach with straight, plain edges? It was downright dull. It may have signified an overly careful approach to the jump. It may also have signaled to the judges, "Here comes a humdinger of a move." But mostly, it showed a failure on the part of the skater to do a creative artistic program.

So, instead of writing rules that squeeze the blood out of the skater, why not write an overall discussion that covers the variety of subjects that cause the rules to be created in the first place? Don't answer that, because it would cause a thinning out of the complicated rules that ultimately keep everything secret, preventing any possibility of another public scandal.

So, the five Program Component Scores (which include their 26 criteria) end up being listed on the TV screen as five marks, which, multiplied by the appropriate factor for whether it is a Short or Long Program, will be added to the total of Technical Scores, which determine the placement of the skater in the competition. These scores are inexplicable to the general audience. It's necessary for the host to say, "She's in second place" or for viewers to see it on the screen to understand what the devil is happening!

Now, you may not agree with the "call" by any particular judge on either the Technical Scores or the Program Component Scores. But listen, buddies! I guarantee you that you won't, because you will not know any judge's call! And if you don't know any judge's call, there ain't no "screaming at the umpire" in this game! So, note the marks that were published for the recent Skate Canada, which show that the second mark Patrick Chan received was a perfect score of 10 for Skating Skills (which is one of the five Program Component Scores . . . remember?)—even though he fell. Anyone who wants to either agree or not agree with this can't yell at the "Umpire" or even at the person sitting in the Judge #2 spot on the judges' dais in the arena who may be recognizable. That's because the second mark announced is not the mark actually awarded by the judge sitting in the #2 spot. The marks are issued in random order, so nobody can know what any judge has actually awarded. This is *secret judging at its best*! The names of the judges with their real marks are kept in a safe in Lausanne and only the General Secretary and a notary can see them, if requested by the Technical Committees.

Holy cow!

Please remember I am not a speed skater, and I don't think or wish that the Fine Art of Figure Skating (or, as other countries call it, Artistic Skating) can or should be judged by measurement alone, which is what is happening.

A summation of this situation is as follows:

1. The judges are disempowered when voting on the Technical Scores.
2. The Technical Controller, Technical Specialist, and the Assistant Technical Specialist have the most control because they set the value of each and every element.

Goodness me!

By the way, there is still another level of control on top of all this. The Technical Committees today also have much less power because all of their decisions or proposals must be approved first by the Chair, Sports Directorate of the ISU, Peter Krick. Peter Krick is a German ex-figure skater and administrator whose reputation is that he is ultra conservative and against any change in the system.

One of the duties of the Technical Committees is to appoint the Referees, the Technical Controllers, and the Technical Specialists for the Championships, the Grand Prix events, and of course the Olympic Games. The Technical Specialists are skating professionals, while the Technical Controllers are ISU Championship judges or Referees.

The Technical Committees have to take into consideration the candidates' experience and their nationalities. The proposals are then reviewed by Peter Krick, who is known to make changes in them. They are then sent to David Dore, the Vice President for Figure Skating (and a former skating force in Canada), who might make some changes. They are then sent on to ISU President Ottavio Cinquanta (whom we have been calling OC), who has the final word. Remember, OC is a speed skater who has no passion for and little understanding of the sport. One has to assume that as he has said, "I know nothing about figure skating," he probably knows little about the qualifications of these individuals, yet he frequently makes changes for one reason or another! Do we need to throw down a flag here, too?

Way back when, I had the fun of meeting Mae West, the rambunctious, funny, notoriously verbally naughty movie star of the Golden Age of film. (If any young twinks sitting on the rug nearby don't know who she is, Google her!) She told the story about a young starlet who, seeing her enormous diamond ring, gushed, "Goodness!"

To which Mae West replied, "Honey, goodness ain't got nuttin' to do with it."

My feeling is that goodness ain't got nuttin' to do with the IJS.

But the IJS does indeed succeed in keeping everyone from knowing what's going on, and the press from celebrating another scandal. Unfortunately, it does not keep the judges from cheating. There are still frequent requests made of judges from judges of other countries! What the IJS does do is make it impossible for anyone to tell if cheating has occurred, which means OC's object to never have another public scandal like the one that happened in Salt Lake City has been accomplished.

Nice going!

As a big aside—this one with a raised eyebrow!— please note that this year, a Ukrainian judge was reported for attempting to influence another judge and was suspended for two years. That situation had quiet publication.

And if you want to raise two eyebrows, I will tell you it's rumored that that Didier Gailhaguet, the mastermind of the French Federation who was convicted and suspended for his role in the 2002 Salt Lake City Scandal, is in the running for the presidency of the ISU in 2016.

Will the shenanigans ever stop?

16 KISS AND CRY...
FIFTEEN SECONDS OF FAME!

Anyone who has watched any figure skating competition, and all of us certainly have, knows what the "Kiss and Cry" is.

But in case any of the dogs on the couch (the animals, that is!) don't know, the Kiss and Cry is that space designated for use immediately after the performance. Competitors are directed up and onto a platform near the door in the hockey barrier where they came off the ice. Here the TV cameras can get close-up shots of the skater (or skaters, if it's an ice dancing or pair skating competition) in their first moments off the ice as they await and receive their marks.

This is also the moment when we should look for "theater." Remember my rant in the Entrances and Exits chapter about post-performance drama? You are very likely to see a "post-performance Performance" here. The pressure is over. Whatever was going to happen, happened. The skaters will be showing their emotions probably more than at any other time.

Sometimes I wring my hands in quiet desperation

about the name Kiss and Cry! It was coined by an elegant lady, Jane Erkko, then president of the Finnish Skating Federation. It correctly sized up the character and goings-on of the Kiss and Cry scene, yet I dislike how the constant references to it fix in the public mind the kind of words that signify the silly aspects of this sport. These are athletes in the aftermath of extreme, sometimes almost heroic, effort. Serious stuff! So I am sorry it was given such a frivolous moniker. But it was a clever description, and it stuck. (So phooey on you, Dick!)

The Kiss and Cry is what has developed from a long history of pursuing what ABC always felt was the essence of sports coverage. That was "The Up Close and Personal" features on athletes—revealing elements of who they were, the story around them, their emotions, their fears, their likes and dislikes.

This principle existed long before television was invented. Sports coverage in newspapers always wanted the story behind the story, the personalization of the great stars. It was about creating heroes every man, woman and child could relate to, admire, envy, applaud, and emulate.

In 1932, the first Olympic Winter Games were held in Lake Placid. This was the one of the first skating events that received major news coverage in America. One sensational story of the event was the glamour of Sonja Henie, the blonde Norwegian cutie-pie who shortened her skirts (a first) and who wore skating boots that were white (a first), orchids on her shoulder (unusual), and always a diamond pin at her throat. Nothing about her was left to chance. She used every second of the moment. For her, it was theater at every step.

There was also the speed skater Irving Jaffee of the United States, (later a sports writer) taking the gold competing in the 5000- and 10,000-meter races. He was confident enough to know that he would win the gold but still asked how to make the win memorable (i.e., be reported with flair and prominence and not listed at the bottom of the page). Someone suggested that he throw himself across the ice when crossing the finish line. It would look like it was a desperate last-minute gesture of Olympian proportions, that he was doing his best to wrest the title away from the thundering pack nipping at his heels. It would be a sensational shot. At the end of the race, he threw himself over the finish line, almost swimming for several yards in Grand Olympic style. The photographers had a field day. No one commented on the fact he was far, far, ahead of the pack and that there was no other skater anywhere near him at the finish. The photo was seen everywhere.

We laughed with him when he told this story on himself.

But it illustrated what Roone Arledge wanted, and that was to tell the story of the athletes and not just the story of who won.

At the 1962 World Figure Skating Championships in Prague, we did the commentary right at the edge of the rink. I was the expert commentator and also did the rinkside interviews. I quickly learned to make the interviewee the focal point. It was the athlete who was the subject of interest, not me as the commentator. I also learned to ask questions that the skater could not answer with a "yes" or a "no".

The point was to capture the immediate, spontaneous moment of ecstasy or agony while the skater was out of breath and not thinking about image control during our interview.

Sometimes the strategy worked. I remember one interview with a champion skater who had totally messed up his program. He knew it, and I knew it, and he knew I knew it! The question I asked was simply, "Well?" He answered with a heartfelt reply of exasperation that never would have been as touching if I had questioned him about what had made him miss that jump.

Sometimes I was the one caught in a spontaneous

moment. I did an interview with Peggy Fleming at the 1964 National Championships in Cleveland. It took place immediately after she had finished her program. She was still breathless. I asked whether a particular move had been difficult. She looked at me and said, "You try it."

It was the best answer possible, and from someone who retained her cool and in the process put down that fellow doing the interview who was a World and Olympic hotshot (he thought!). I'd broken two of my cardinal rules of interviewing. First: I'd asked a question that could be answered by a "yes" or "no". Secondly, it was a stupid question.

Later on, when Peggy Fleming and I were doing commentary together, she delighted in putting a tape over my mouth on camera to shut me up. (Now, don't anybody make a comment, because whatever you say, someone else has already said it!)

This process of my doing rinkside interviews immediately following a skater's performance eventually stopped. The producers were exasperated by my constantly dropping the microphone on the desk when an interview was called. I was too zeroed in on the question I would ask and forgot the crackling noise the mike would make when it was dropped.

The need to have immediacy in seeing the skaters' reactions post-performance eventually morphed into the "Kiss and Cry" station.

So, what happens? First, the skater(s) will sit down, usually on a square box covered with carpeting. The fellow will sit with his knees wide apart (a guy thing); the girl will sit with her knees close together (a girl thing). Maybe the coach or choreographer will sneak in beside them so they can hug or kiss them, or cheer and cry with them. Some skaters express their emotional reaction to the marks or to the whole scene, and it usually comes straight from the heart.

Sometimes they pull on an ear to signal to a friend

that they are thinking of them.

But note the way everyone acts and is dressed. Some of the coaches show up with so many tags on their necks, they look like they have passes to the U.S. Mint. Others sometimes look as if they were out for stroll, going to the local pub, or about to clean up the cellar. Some look sharp! The skaters, particularly if they are sweating (which is not unusual, considering their efforts), frequently pull on a jacket to ward off any cool drafts, but in doing so often pull on some advertisement over an elegant costume. Swan feathers do not look good under a sweat jacket!

Then some of the skaters swig from a bottle of water. Some show every emotion ever displayed at The Actors Studio. Some of the entourage are self-effacing, quiet, laid-back, and above the turmoil, recognizing that it is the skater's moment and not theirs. Some paw the faces of their pupils and fawn over them. Some overly relish their fifteen seconds of fame.

Don't misunderstand. Everyone has the right to react differently. Remember, this is an emotional moment for all. It is the culmination of a lot of time, effort, and energy on the part of the skaters, their coaches, and parents.

Sometimes a skater will use the moment to express a flair that would not otherwise get into their performance. Johnny Weir, for example, usually skated in a more-or-less quiet costume. Elsewhere, he might show up in clothes that were over the top, but never in a competition. He was too smart for that, knowing that Rule #500 (I call it the "Costume Rule") disapproved of garish or "theatrical" clothing. At one championship he waited until the Kiss and Cry, and then put on his head a ring of red roses, which I've said earlier looked something like a crown of roses or maybe a crown of thorns.

At the forthcoming Olympic Winter Games, there is a new team competition being held between ten teams. It has been announced that there will be ten Kiss and Cry stations.

I can't wait!

In the end, the Kiss and Cry, that weakly named element in the story of figure skating, does provide a purpose. It is sometimes an irritating purpose but nevertheless a purpose: it lets us see the skater up close and personal, at least for a moment.

17 YOU'VE GOT PERSONALITY

In the 1950s, Lloyd Price and Harold Logan wrote a song called "Personality." It was probably the song with the least amount of personality I have heard. But the idea was good, so I hope we all remember it when while we are watching Olympic and other skating events. You never know when you will come up smack-dab, face-to-face with something or someone that stops you in your tracks.

What is "personality"? Is it what the rules call "Performance"? Is it what's known as "presence," or maybe the impact one makes upon entering a room? Is it the ability to feel and communicate powerful emotion? An actor wants to have it all: personality, impact, presence, and emotion.

Personality is only revealed by those who are capable of showing it. Can they open up their heart and permit the audience see what they are feeling, thinking, wanting or not wanting.

In 1951 during my junior year at Harvard, the musical *The King and I* opened. It came to the Schubert Theatre in Boston on a tryout run before the Broadway opening. It starred the English actress Gertrude Lawrence, who played Anna. She had been given the "Woman of the Year" award by the Hasty Pudding-Institute of 1770 (one of the oldest theatrical and social clubs in America), and a few of us went to the second night, bringing flowers in her honor.

Oscar Hammerstein, who wrote the lyrics to Richard Rodgers's music, was at first reluctant to take on the production, feeling that Lawrence, who had not performed in many musicals, wasn't known as a great singer—and of greater concern was her reputation for "diva-like behavior." He needn't have worried. She had a dazzling radiance, bringing, as he later commented, a "magic light onstage." Call it personality, presence, impact, or star quality—she had it. When we went backstage to present her the flowers, she showed even in her dressing room an incredible luminescence. I never forgot the aura she projected.

(As another of my favorite asides, I hesitate to tell you that when Gertrude Lawrence won the "Woman of the Year" award, I was playing in the annual Hasty Pudding musical at Harvard which that year was called *Buddha Knows Best*. Each year the production was written and directed by members of the Club. At that time both the Club and Harvard were all-male, which meant that men played the female roles as well as the male ones. I played a Nubian slave girl who sang a song that went like this: "All you need is a light in your eye to light the way to love." The late Fred Gwynne, who later starred in the TV series *The Munsters*, played the explorer.

He was superb.

I was not.)

During summer vacation of my second year at Harvard Law School, I was sent on a trip through the Far East in order to make connections for a new company my brothers and I had started. I stopped in Los Angeles, where I visited Jules Stein, the personable head of Music Corporation of America (MCA), the largest talent agency at the time, which much later became NBC Universal and is now Comcast. We stood at the top of the magnificent curving white marble staircase in the entrance hall of his office saying goodbye when suddenly a man bolted up the stairs three steps at a time. He was tanned and had electric blue eyes. Stein said, "Clark, I want you to meet Dick Button." The man thrust out his hand and said, "Nice to meet you, Dick; I'm a great fan of yours." I stood there shaking the hand of Clark Gable. I was speechless, not because either his recognition nor his performance as an actor playing Rhett Butler in *Gone With the Wind* had made him the most popular movie star in America, but because of the overwhelming charisma he projected. Like Gertrude Lawrence, it was as if he had an inner beacon.

Some skaters have that inner light. Some may project it in high voltage; others in softer tones. Janet Lynn had it in a gentle, soft, blond way. Katarina Witt oozed it. Stephanie Rosenthal skated in the 2006 National Championships with such abandon, joy, and lack of restraint that she enveloped the audience in her musical freedom. Her skating was a combination of hip-hop and street dance and called for standing ovations. It was a refreshing moment that glowed. She was not technically as advanced as some others, but she represented what has now almost been lost in the competitive world, where the parameters of "Technical Merit" have overwhelmed Artistic Impression. Stephanie Rosenthal showed that, as I later was quoted, "we have lost the ability not to be so scared of getting off-centered."

Remember the Program Component Scores we talked about in chapter 15? (If you don't, you are excused, because they all mix together). One of them is titled "Performance/Execution"—and please don't tell me you already forgot that!

"Performance/Execution" is judged according to nine criteria, which are (and I quote):

- Physical, emotional and intellectual involvement;
- Carriage;
- Style and individuality/personality;

- Clarity of movement;
- Variety and contrast;
- Projection;
- Unison and "oneness" (Pair Skating)
- Balance in performance (Pair Skating)
- Spatial awareness between partners – management of the distance between partners and management of changes of hold (Pair Skating).

Personality is thus valued as only one-half of one of the nine criteria. Also, if you stop to think about it, execution and performance are two different things. Maybe that's why these rules are so dense and hard to understand. Even the doggies don't get it!

"Performance" can take any and all forms and may surprise you when you least expect it. What is unfortunate is when a skater has no sense of performance, little impact, not much presence, and minimal personality.

The skaters we remember over the years are the ones whose style, enthusiasm, *personality*, sudden blast of something, or subtlety, musicality, restraint, or just plain old fuss and feathers can leave you speechless, as ice dancers Torvill and Dean did in each of the years leading up to the 1984 Olympics with programs like Mack and Mabel, Barnum, and the Paso Doble (if you don't remember, look them up on YouTube).

In their case, it could have been called the Personality of Choreography. They hardly ever cracked a facial expression and never deviated from their absolute focus on the intent of the program. As a result, we were immediately drawn into their world, into their presence, despite the fact that they ignored us completely. Moving within the hypnotic music of *Bolero*, they seemed almost entranced—and so were we. They made an indelible impact.

To be honest with you, my friends here on the couch, I am not interested in seeing nice skating or skating that is "pleasant." What I want most of all is to see and feel the impact of a strong emotion. What does the skater feel about the music, and how does he or she show us what that feeling is? This is theater, baby! And don't you forget it unless you're a speed skater, where the audience only needs to know how far, how fast, what the ruler counts or what the timer says, or how many beans are in the pot, and everyone gets their kicks out of seeing a record made.

Make no mistake, many athletes do provide great impact through their physical achievement. Whether long track speed skater Eric Heiden at the 1984 Olympic Winter Games ever realized it or not, the way he moved like greased lightning was electrifying. Seeing boxer Muhammad Ali in the ring was indeed like seeing the both the flight of a butterfly and the attack of a bee. Short track speed skater Apolo Ohno showed cat-like agility and extraordinary personality during *Dancing with the Stars*. Like Kristi Yamaguchi, who exuded the greatest amount of personality I have seen her show in winning *Dancing with the Stars*, it almost seemed as if it took another medium to bring it out.

While I was in the Burke Rehabilitation Center recovering from the fall I told you about in chapter 8, I watched (instead of attending) the 2001 World Figure Skating Championships in Vancouver. For the first time in years, I saw it first on TV.

That was the first time I registered the performance of the Russian skater Evgeni Plushenko. I was mesmerized. He did truly magnificent jumps but was a mediocre spinner. He also stood around a lot wiggling. He was almost arrogant, famously attacking incidental movements and endlessly posing. I could not stop watching.

Later he went on to win a gold medal at the 2006 Olympic Winter Games in Torino. At the 2010 Olympics Winter Games in Vancouver, he won the silver medal, losing to Evan Lysacek. Pouting, he criticized Evan for not doing a quadruple jump, stating that anyone who did not do a quad should have skated in the ladies' event. He apparently forgot that Evan won the title fairly under the new rules—not my favorite rules, but they were the rules. Yet despite this immaturity, Plushenko had pizzazz. He was a bundle of friction. He showed his emotions and what he was feeling.

If someone is difficult, that's OK with me. I may not think it's nice or correct or polite, but it certainly makes for interesting theater. I am not interested in seeing folks who skate "nicely." Give me raw feelings anytime, even though I may elsewhere in the work espouse subtle positions, clean endings, or even highly controlled movements. That goes to show you there are multiple feelings and reactions we all have about every aspect of the performance level of this most interesting of all sports.

I have to back off this opinion in the case of Tonya Harding, who was accused of being knowledgeable about her husband's involvement in a plan to have Nancy Kerrigan whacked in the knee at the National Championships and before the 1994 Winter Olympics. Intentionally injuring someone else is never something to condone. As an aside, Tonya Harding was later banned for life by the ISU. Judges who have been convicted of cheating are, after a short suspension, often back judging. How about that for consistency?

Tonya was the first American female figure skater to do a triple Axel. She was a stocky powerhouse who had sophisticated support from Seattle skating enthusiasts, but even with that she always seemed to make the wrong decisions. Everyone and his brother watched the skating events that followed, where the resulting emotions ran high and every one of the top skaters showed their feelings. Once again, it was raw theater.

There is theater all around the world of skating, and it both influences many of us and appears in many forms and styles.

Come to think of it, it is difficult now for skaters to achieve a sense of much emotion because the technical requirements are so massive. Some skaters are capable of it, but many are submerged in the morass of point-getting. Still, many skaters learn ways to gather their talents and move them into the spotlight. (OK, so I know there are no spotlights in a competition. That's just a metaphor!) There are several who have become different and better skaters (and performers) as they themselves changed.

Scott Hamilton was one. He always wanted to be thought of as a sportsman and even went so far as to have a costume made for the 1984 Olympic Winter Games in Sarajevo (where he won a gold medal) that looked somewhat like a speed skater's or a skier's body-hugging unitard.

He frequently said he was not an artist, but I was once quoted as saying, "whether he liked to admit it or not, he was an artist." Later, as an exhibition and professional skater, he always gave "performances" that were entertaining and filled with humor, letting his emotions show. It was interesting to watch him change and develop both as a performer and as an individual.

Brian Boitano and Rudy Galindo were two skaters who famously and publicly developed their impact, their "performance."

Brian lost the 1987 World Championships in Cincinnati, coming in second. The problem was, he looked like a teenager who been dropped in a vat of silver (he hadn't, but his silver costume made it look that way) and skated a program that was mechanically switch-backed (whatever that means!). Backstage after the competition, I made the suggestion that he find a choreographer who would give him several different programs—a tango, a jazz a waltz, whatever—as long as each one was different! Then he should throw them away and start a new program. The idea was that he needed to stretch his imagination, develop new moves, and experience different emotions.

He found Canadian pair champion and choreographer Sandra Bezic, who revamped his entire persona. He let his hair grow out and developed a new program. All of which converted him from a gawky teenager into a romantic leading man in the space of a year. Sandra was the perfect choice to guide him, and he was able to absorb and complete the picture he wanted to paint. A year after losing in Cincinnati, he won the 1988 Olympic gold medal.

Rudy Galindo came from another scene. He had won titles in both single and pair skating (with Kristi Yamaguchi). But skating two events can be taxing and double the amount of expense, concentration, coaching, and practice. Kristi elected to move into singles only.

That left Rudy somewhat high and dry, even though he had been doing singles. The problem was, Rudy had obstacles to deal with. He had not been born into a well-off family. He had lost a brother and a coach to AIDS. He was an Hispanic in a mostly-WASP world. He was gay in a world where homosexuality was not yet more or less accepted. It was not an impressive springboard from which to continue skating.

What he did have going for himself was a dedication and enthusiasm for the sport that was irresistibly powerful. Even more important, he had a vision of where he wanted to go. And most valuable of all, he had a sense of theater, a sense of humor, and the ability to show his emotions.

(On a side note, his sister became his "Skating Mother," guiding and supporting him and coaching him into the right edges of life. "Skating Mothers" is a marvelous subject, but it will only appear in Volume Two of *Push Dick's Button*!)

These qualities resulted in two extremely successful but wildly different programs. In one, he took on the role of von Rothbart, the evil character in *Swan Lake*. Galindo's tightly clipped, narrowly cut, dark beard presented the menacing villain. His performance also succeeded in embodying the basic requirement needed for anyone to take on a role from one of the most famous ballets that comes with a long history: the ability to meet the physical requirements of the dance style. This was not a role for a smooth, smiling Fred Astaire or the down-and-dirty style of tap dancer Savion Glover (unless one wanted to take the character of von Rothbart into another realm, which would be an interesting reach, indeed).

Instead, Rudy clearly embraced the classical style of *Swan Lake* that has been traditional among dancers performing in *Swan Lake* for more than a century. It was inspired by the noble elegance visible in the movements of swans—the curve, arch, and stretch of their necks. This was no place for a relaxed-shoulders look or a shallow sense of one's presence. How often do we see women skaters in white costumes with white feathers, imitating in the most casual of positions the swan's movements? Just the slightest comparison with the rendering of *Swan Lake* by any major ballet company will magnify the disparity.

Rudy Galindo took on the history of *Swan Lake*. He followed the classical line in his choreography and displayed stretched and pointed feet throughout, including on catchfoots that were (or should be) the envy of both male and female skaters everywhere today. He enveloped himself in the evil character of von Rothbart and in the classical style that was appropriate for and demanded by the story, history, and choreography of *Swan Lake*.

Galindo's performance epitomizes the totality of all the elements that should go into a performance. The concept, the music, the costume, the choreography, and the execution must all be in sync. That was the case in the *Bolero* by T and D (see chapter 4 for *that* story!), *Prelude to the Afternoon of a Faun* by John Curry, *Swan Lake* by Ludmila Belousova and Oleg Protopopov (and by Rudy Galindo, as just mentioned), and in riveting performances by many others who grasped the essence of painting whatever picture they desired to create.

205

The second performance by Galindo that reached this level was an exhibition. It was to "YMCA" sung by the Village People. Here again Galindo got the picture. He used humor and made fun of himself. He mimicked the characters who sang the song, an obvious take-off on gay life. It was an incredibly successful performance, became a favorite program of the audience, and was demanded by the producers of every show he was invited to be in.

What's the point of this tirade? First, that having impact, presence, and personality is not a question of what picture one picks, but of whether one embraces it fully, envelops oneself in it, and plays it to the utmost. And second, that the current rule of "Performance/Execution" should be made a major element in the judging. If you see it in speed skaters, it is usually when their personality comes out in their interviews and public life, but it has little to do with their winning their race, which is a pure measurement of time. Figure skating, in contrast, needs personality built into the act itself. The rules need to more adequately address this.

Personality can be seen in a skater like Peggy Fleming, who rarely smiled and seldom flailed about, but who skated with elegance and simplicity. (But of course that was when you didn't have to stuff your program so full of arm movements and doodads that your arms, legs, and entire body resembled a batch of live spaghetti worming its way around a bowl!)

Personality was certainly inherent in Midori Ito. This young lady was a charmer, a likeable little Miss Sunshine. She was not blessed with long legs or an "Amazonian" body. But when she stepped on the ice, it seemed as if she welcomed us into her space. In the 1991 World Championship, she skated a dazzling Lutz combination that was high and long and would have been perfect had she not skated too close to the barrier and flown through the opening that had been cut out for the TV camera. Falling in front of the camera, she nevertheless, and like the great champion she was, picked herself up, rushed back onto the ice, and kept on skating.

But at the end of her performance, and in the true Japanese tradition of politeness, she skated over to the spot where she had crashed into the camera and bowed politely to both the Referee, Benjamin Wright, and to the cameraman, apologizing for entering their space!

It became an iconic gesture of respect and politeness. It was personality personified.

I suppose personality was built into the French skater Surya Bonaly who, when she didn't like her placement at a competition, took off the silver medal that had been placed around her neck and hurled it away (granted, not the best way to display personality), and also, to show her disgust and in defiance of the rules, deliberately did a back flip (which is not allowed in the free program!), which landed on *one* foot (very difficult!), giving the audience, the judges, and the "system" a clear picture of her opinion. There were many different reactions, but whatever you may think, it was fun to see and certainly got notice.

I can talk 'til a snowball lives in Hades, but as you can see, personality is not something one can easily describe. It can appear in everything from the concept to the choreography to the performance to the pure creative force of any skater. It can appear in charm, wit, joy, and temper. It is Katarina Witt exuding enough charm to lure the devil from his lair. It is Dorothy Hamill squinting and shrugging her shoulders in disbelief and modesty at even holding a medal. It is Tenley Albright choosing to skate a backward "Shoot the Duck" that then rises up into a back spiral, when most skaters considered a "Shoot the Duck" to be a move so beneath the radar that only swamp skaters would do it.

(An aside: A Shoot the Duck entailed skating forward in a simple sitting position on one foot with the other leg held straight ahead and off the ice, like the barrel of a gun—thus "Shoot the Duck"! Got it?). Many started to ridicule her but stopped when they saw how effective it was.

It was also Tenley Albright when she did one of the simplest of jumps that normally doesn't get a second glance (nor a single point under the current rules), which is called a mazurka jump. A mazurka jump is a straight up toe pick jump with crossed feet and no turns at all. The effect she achieved was like a taut, stretched exclamation point that was filled with tension. It wasn't just the jump, but her total physical and mental commitment to it that exuded personality: the stretch, the pull up of the body, the pointed feet, and the *ballon*/suspension she achieved. I always said I would rather see one move done beautifully than ten moves done sloppily.

It can be Brian Boitano skating one of the finest spread eagles, where you could have placed a six-foot steel ruler the length of his body from head to toe, so straight and perfect was the position.

It was Michelle Kwan doing a rink-long change-of-edge spiral with the most charming of smiles that warmed our hearts. It was also Michelle Kwan answering the question which of how she felt losing the gold medal to Tara Lipinski, saying, "I didn't lose the gold, I won the silver."

Personality can erupt anywhere—during a performance, immediately afterwards, in the Kiss and Cry, or on the medal podium. It is a matter of letting your emotions be seen, and that can happen anywhere and at any time.

I guess my favorite explosion of emotion (personality?) happened with the Italian ice dancers Barbara Fusar-Poli and Maurizio Margaglio. At the 2006 Olympic Winter Games in Torino, he lost control while supporting her in a waist-high horizontal position dance move and dropped her flat as a pancake on the ice. She was furious. She stared him down, wouldn't speak to him, slapped him, and made him skate their program without looking at him . . . generally making herself out to be the wicked witch of Portofino.

I am describing moments of flair and drama and pizzazz, some of which are not worth their weight in salt. But others are worth their weight in gold—as medals, as memories, or both. The main point is that "personality" should be evident in the performance itself. Not just in antics before or afterwards. It isn't always in the cards for some skaters to show their personality through their emotions—Torvill and Dean let their skating do the talking. But it is these moments, as well as the unusual, the interesting, and the different sparks, that we remember over the years and reminisce about on the couch as we fight over the last bits of popcorn and debate the marks of the latest skater to pass through the Kiss and Cry. It is what makes figure skating the fascinating sport and art that it is.

And it is the lack of these moments in skating today that I feel is causing audiences to have less interest in watching skating. Failed attempt after failed attempt to do a quad is not a sign of personality. Both performance and personality are key factors in attracting audiences. Variety of styles, flair, and pizzazz are essential. Maybe keep something like a Short Program as a Technical Program for the measured elements (as long as you don't give points for falls), but leave the Long Program as an Artistic Program to showcase the flair and personality of figure skating. This would allow two programs that are different: one that emphasizes measurement, and the other that is infused with theater, personality, and spark—which would restore the creative enthusiasm for all of us who love the Fine Art of Figure Skating.

18 LIKES, DISLIKES, AND FAVORITES

As an old codger who has been around since forever, I can't forget some of the best and some of the worst things I have seen over the years. And even though some of them may have happened long before most of you were old enough to drink beer, let alone Mother's milk, I still enjoy remembering them. There may be no rhyme but plenty of reason for liking or disliking certain moves in skating. Also, as the title of this chapter says, there are certain moves that become favorites to watch or for the skater to do. They become favorites because the skater does them well or because the audience *likes and applauds them*, and they become trademarks for a skater.

So come with me and let's tap dance through some of the things in some performances, competitions, or exhibitions that dazzled us and some that turned us off. (And if this doesn't interest you, I will understand completely if we order Chinese instead.)

Since jumps are the current name of the game in competitive skating, watch for one particular jump and its variations, some of which seem to have slipped between the cracks in the ice. That is the split jump.

Splits are spectacular when done well.

211

All too often they are not done well.

I worked hard to get a good split. During the summer, daytime practice sessions at the 1932 Olympic Arena in Lake Placid were extremely crowded and the ice was badly rutted, so I always slept late and skated late at night when the ice was empty. I would commandeer my mother to sit up in the lounge behind the glass windows. She was always knitting something or other. When I practiced splits, I would signal up to her to ask how far the split was split. She would hold up her knitting needles, positioning them to indicate how far I had stretched.

It took a lot of knitting and a long time before I eventually achieved the full split I wanted. (As an aside, I learned much later that my mother did not always take her eyes off the knitting and fairly often had not even seen the splits I was practicing, but always kept the needles short of a full split. She knew what I was pushing for and wanted to support my dedication to my goal. Talk about "Skating Mothers"!)

The position I wanted, I learned later, was called a *grand jeté* in ballet. In this position the front leg and foot are stretched forward with the foot perpendicular or slightly to the side while the back leg and foot are turned flat and thus parallel to the ice. The hips face in the direction the dancer (skater) is moving. Katherine Healy (a skater and a ballerina of the first order) performed a beautiful *grand jeté* split.

There were some sensational split jumps in slightly varying positions in skating in the 1940s, 1950s, and later, by skaters like Sonya Klopfer Dunfield, Cathy Machado, Aja Zanova, Joe Marshall, Tom McGinnis, and Belita Jepson-Turner (called simply "Belita," this remarkable lady was an Olympic competitor(1936), movie and stage actress, and ballerina who brought superb line and dance qualities to her skating).

As time went on, a different split became popular, and it's the one that is almost always performed today.

This is the "Russian split." This was a traditional folk dance move that was made even more popular in the 1960s by the Moiseyev Dance Company, a dance troupe established by choreographer Igor Moiseyev that had a repertoire based primarily on folk dancing. It was interesting that one of his first ballets was titled *The Footballer.* The company presented folk dances that were acrobatic, energetic, often humorous, and extremely theatrical.

In a Russian split, the dancer jumps from a standing position facing the audience and opens both legs to the right and left in a split, with both legs parallel to the ground. Imagine sitting on the edge of a chair and stretching your legs in front of you so your torso and your legs are at 90-degree angles. The legs are split as wide apart as possible, with the hips facing the audience. The trick here is that it requires extreme stretching to achieve a full Russian "split" position.

The difference between the dancer and the skater doing this move is that a dancer does the split from a standstill, facing the audience, while the skater is always moving and has an audience all the way around.

The problem with Russian splits is that most skaters simply do not split fully enough. They take the easier route and get the legs up, but not in a full split. Take a look at some film of the Moiseyev Dance Company in action and see the applause-getting, rapid repetitions of Russian splits that their stars perform. They can be sensational. The other problem is that because a skater is moving, it is most likely that the split is also seen from either one end or the other and not from the full front. Unfortunately, those views clearly show when a skater has taken the easier (not the full split) position. Some skaters do get it right. Note Sasha Cohen's Russian splits, which are dramatically split. Sasha's mother was a dancer and knew the importance of stretching to the ultimate.

The split I did early on was a hybrid split: Russian

hips (facing the audience) and *grand jeté* legs. Was I a mixed-up kid, or what? Later, I was photographed at the Wollman Rink in New York City's Central Park doing what had morphed into a Russian split. It had great stretch and was an excellent split jump, even if I do say so myself. Good, Dick!

Still later, however, I found myself doing an easier and lazier version of a Russian split, which was not as much of a split as I had achieved earlier. Not good, Dick!

Many skaters today do flying sit spins. But they are not flying sit spins that do much flying. Instead they are small jumps where the pull-up of the leg into a sitting position in the air is not much higher than the body would be in if the skater weren't jumping at all. I wonder whether any of the Technical Specialists or the judges have ever seen a superb flying sit spin that really flies.

I have, but it was a long time ago. In the 1951 World Figure Skating Championships in Milan, Hayes Jenkins (who was to win the 1956 Olympic gold medal) skated to *Hungarian Rhapsody*, and at the end in the most dramatic climax of the music roared down the ice in sweeping back edges, cross cut around the end of the rink, and let loose with a flying sit spin that did indeed soar. The audience leaned forward to watch. He had originally been taught by Gustave Lussi to jump up and forward into the sitting position. He did, and this flying sit spin flew up and forward. Lussi also taught that, as the skater rose into the air, he was to simultaneously pull up his skating leg so that his body took a helicopter position in the air, where the back was forward and the body and legs were compressed, much like a cannonball position in a sit spin. The trick was to keep your upper body far forward so you didn't straighten up and when landing and sit back down on the ice. (Remember when Janet Lynn at the 1972 Winter Olympics sat down on her flying sit spin?) At the peak of the jump, the skater was to lower the skating leg like a landing wheel.

This talk about helicopters and landing wheels is maybe a little odd for skaters, but as was usual with Lussi, his analogies were visual, clear, and understandable. He was an articulate and artful communicator.

This climactic moment by Hayes Jenkins was one of the greatest flying moments in a flying spin I have seen. It makes it difficult for me watch the ditsy little pip-squeak jumps we see today. I also doubt whether many folk recognize what I am talking about or have seen a truly spectacular flying sit spin. Oh, well; that's one of the hazards of getting old!

Spirals can be elegant, humorous, dramatic, and powerful. There are endless varieties, including forward and backward, inside and outside edge, front and back catchfoots, spirals and pair spirals, and death spirals which have so many different variations (where entrances can have forward, backward, inside, and outside edges) and most of which, it seems, were invented by the Protopopovs.

Back a ways, pair skaters got into the habit during a death spiral of allowing the lady to arch back and get so low to the ice that her head would sweep the ice and snow would accumulate on her hair. It was fun to see and it amused the audience. Then it was deemed "Not Good" and "Not suitable for the Fine Art of Figure Skating" and would be marked down. It was fun while it lasted. It didn't hurt anyone, but still went the way of the dodo.

There is one particular spiral that I admire and that is seldom seen today. It's a man's spiral and was popularized by Gillis Grafström, the Swedish three-time Olympic champion. He was an architect, married to Cécile "Baby" Grafström, who was a descendent of the composer Felix Mendelssohn. Together they collected skating artwork and memorabilia that later became the core holdings of the World Figure Skating Museum and Hall of Fame in Colorado Springs, Colorado. In 1947, when she was downsizing, Cécile Grafström offered to sell the entire collection. My father said that if I would like it, he would buy it for me. And I said, with the stupidity of youth, "What will I do with all those dusty old things?" Mrs. Grafström gave me an eighteenth-century Dutch tile of a skater. I then started a lifetime of collecting the art of skating, yet never equaled the collection I could have had in one fell swoop.

Gillis Grafström was a specialist in skating elaborate figures. I have film of him in the 1920s and 1930s showing him doing the most elaborate figures possible with three turns, brackets, counters, cross cuts, changes of edges, and all manner of curlicues, turns, and movements.

The spiral I referred to earlier can be seen in an iconic picture of him taken outdoors in the Alps. He is doing a forward inside spiral with a truly strong lean of the body. (Remember, everyone, "an edge is created by a lean of the body".) In this photo, his free leg and skating leg are both bent. The arms are to the back. He is both skating and looking straight at the camera. The position of that spiral is Art Moderne in feeling, and exceptionally stylish. It reminds one of the Demetre Chiparus sculptures of the 1920s. There's a photo of me doing it if I can find it. I regret we don't see this particular spiral done today.

I have so often railed against things like loose laces, sloppy laybacks, rounded shoulders and legs and feet that were not stretched and pointed that I will not bore you by repeating those rants. But I will rev up my vocal cords again for the subject of flailing arms, head bops, unnecessary waist drops, and all sorts of little dips and dewdrops that skaters do in order to get a few more points. They do them because the rules ask for more and more, but it's like trying to spice up an omelet by throwing too much pepper on it because you don't know what herbs to sprinkle lightly. Wasn't it Diana Vreeland, the guru of high fashion, who said, "A little bad taste is like a nice splash of paprika"? So, maybe a few dips and bobbles are OK, but let's not burn the omelet with a fiery overdose of the red stuff.

For anyone who might be asking, the reason for the original levels that are awarded to each move (see chapter 15 for a gallop through the new skating rules . . . then again, maybe you should just keep reading) is to put pressure on coaches and choreographers to make everything more and more difficult (these levels are good for rewarding revolutions in jumps. Spins, on the other hand, are now so convoluted with varieties of positions that they no longer look like spins). But the new rules are increasing neither the quality nor the standard of figure skating. The new rules reward what a few speed skaters think constitutes quality and standards. The sole aim of speed skating is to go faster (unless you are trying to have a leisurely afternoon gliding from one spot to another on the Rideau Canal in Ottawa). "Going faster" in speed skating shouldn't be equated with cramming more unnecessary filler movements in figure skating.

And now, as I hear it, there is a Level 5 being pushed. That might mean still higher marks for adding still another position to a spin, which is already so jiggledied up you can't see the spin for the trees. (Sorry for the mixed metaphor!)

And while I am at it (oh, boy, Dick; why not go and have a decaf to slow down your adrenaline?), let me tell you what is in my "hope-for" column. OC (remember, that's Ottavio Cinquanta, the former speed skater who is president of the ISU) wants to reduce the expenses for competitions. So he is suggesting and looking for ways to have both men and women compete against each other. Now, the editorial he wrote that I read was in the official bulletin of the ISU. It did not specify whether this goal was for speed skating events or figure skating events, but then it also did not say whether it was intended for both, which suggests that maybe someone should have specified which. But now it has been announced that there will be a team figure skating competition between teams made up of men, ladies, pair, and dance couples, just before but as part of the Olympic Winter Games in Sochi.

Competitions including men and women together is a zip dinger of an idea! It will certainly cut costs, and I can just see the guys doing catchfoot diddly, and . . . but no, let's not go there! At least it will bring some country and many skaters a slew of more gold medals!

Which brings me to another of my snarky little "likes and dislikes" (but which also can be a favorite), and that's spread eagles. The point here is simple. If you have a body that can achieve a "flat" line, use it. Heck, flaunt it!

How many skaters who are Olympic champions simply never could achieve a great spread eagle? I won't mention them, because I would have to include myself. So if you don't have a "flat as a ruler" body, try to stick to a straight line or an inside edge spread eagle. The lean into or the straight up position can hide a lot of bumps that would otherwise appear.

For a welcome aside, see Brian Boitano's spread eagle. It's the best! And also a favorite for him!

(With all this talk on the couch about food and spread eagles, I want to assure you that you will never see a Battle between these Bs (Boitano and Button!): neither a Battle of Cooking nor a Battle of Spread Eagling. I don't cook, and my spread eagle was an inside one. Enough said?)

Sonja Henie had several moves that were distinctively her own favorites, and she always did them in her movies: running on her toes; fast, deep forward-leaning speed stroking, and a half Lutz. She also was noted for very long straight up spins, wearing a costume that included a tall feather on the top of her head. (I suspect a little film repetition and some faster film speed, too, enhanced the length and speed of these spins.) She also popularized black ice.

Now, anyone today who thinks black ice is that one-inch expanse of ice that appears in the winter on highways is woefully misled. That should be called "dangerous ice," because it can cause terrible car accidents and pileups. Real black ice is what forms on a pond, lake, or glacier; is thick enough to take the weight of skaters; and has never been skated on or snowed on. Once it has been skated on or has had snow become imbedded in it, the ice must melt all the way through and then refreeze to create a thickness that will hold all of us folks who lust for it. The blackness comes from the dark brown, almost black base of the pond or lake that shows through the clear ice, making it appear to be almost black. Skating on it is delicious and leaves the sharpest white edges, like chalk marks on a blackboard.

I occasionally get black ice on the pond at my farm in upstate New York, which, by the way, is called Ice Pond Farm.

(Since this is a conversation, I will add another aside! Ice was cut from this pond in the nineteenth century and stored in an ice house, which still exists on the property. Ice cutting was a major industry, and the prints and newspaper clippings of the period show its magnitude. OK, guys! I am not that old that I spent my time cutting ice in my youth. A few cubes in a glass are OK, though I still call my refrigerator an icebox from the days when the ice man delivered ice. Good grief! Is it time to again recall the old Amish saying, "Too soon oldt, too late schmart"?)

Other "favorites," in addition to Brian Boitano's spread eagle, are clearly Michelle Kwan's inside-outside smiling spiral (I can still see her beaming in my mind's eye), Sasha Cohen's Russian split, Alexei Yagudin's forward toe stamping runs, Ronnie Robertson's knee rolls, Charlotte's Charlotte Stop, and Aja Zanova in Ice Follies doing a great split and also a long-legged walk down endless stairs draped in what almost seemed like nothing more than a feather boa . . . and if I could please have another schnapps with my hot dog I could go on forever!

But let me stop and go back to Ronnie Robertson's knee rolls. These were done in a sitting position with both knees together. They were done with extremely fast turns and traveled with the speed of lightning across the ice. They always got the audience going. Now, that's a good idea for replacing Twizzles. I have seen others do knee rolls since, but no one seems to get it quite right or fast enough.

Sorry again, but I forgot to tell you about my pet dislike for Twizzles. I see nothing glamorous or interesting about a Twizzle. It usually calls for up to five three turns on one foot followed by the same number of three turns on the other foot. I have seldom seen it done with elegance or excitement. It is nothing more than a required, almost circus-like balancing move—except that in the circus, which is all about entertaining people, it would be changed to something else and made exciting. Under the rules, it is simply another way to demand some more points, yet does little more than test you to see if you will catch an edge and go Plop! (At least that could be entertaining!) Davis and White do it beautifully, but it is still not a beautiful move.

In my humble opinion, a Twizzle is simply a less athletic, less exciting, less interesting move similar to a balancing act. Let skaters do it if it contributes toward some choreographic interest—which should be the skaters' and the choreographers' choice. If necessary, put it in the Short Program and forget rewarding it in the Long Program.

So many moves were immortalized in the ice shows that are not allowed in competitive skating. That's something of a pity because many of the ice shows are no longer in existence, and it's the competitions that have been televised and are the most-watched skating events. (That's not as true as it used to be, because now most of the events, such as the 2013 World Figure Skating Championships, weren't even on a U.S. television network this past year except for a belated summary show.)

It's almost as if the current rules, which measure

everything, can't figure out how to reward a slide on the ice, or an airplane spin, or any other of the "show" moves. Maybe it's just because they are too showy and us "higher level" folks consider them beneath us! A back flip is a gymnastic move, and it is disallowed in skating competitions. Triple and quadruple jumps are vertical gymnastic moves, but they are encouraged. A Twizzle is a gymnastic balance beam move and is encouraged. Why aren't we recognizing that the current rules are leaning toward a gymnastic type of competition for skating, where the quad and multi-convoluted spins are simply replacing the tumbling acts in a gymnastics floor exercise and Twizzles replace the turns on a balance beam?

We don't always need to know the technical details to know that a skater has performed a difficult but artistically beautiful move. Despite my kvetching, when almost any move is done exceptionally well, it is inspiring. We don't always need to have a move that is so intricate it takes more than half a page to describe. When something is great, we know it. Excellence has staying power.

Remember when Emanuel Sandhu, the Canadian figure skater who was also a dancer of note, did a "broken body spin" where he kept both his skating leg and his free leg straight—and then, while spinning, dropped the upper half of his body down so his head was close to his feet? It was a crisp, sharp position that was striking to see. When others do this spin, they just appear to be sticking their fannies in the air. That may be striking, too, but for other reasons. Where are you, Charlie Cyr, talking about crotch shots, et cetera, when we need you?

When all's said and done, remember that the two themes of technical merit and artistic impression go hand in hand. As the song "Love and Marriage" says, "you can't have one without the other."

19 WHERE DO WE GO FROM HERE?

The first thing we do, I guess, is zip down through some years of history and retrace our figures!

Way back in the 1930s, my parents sent my two brothers and me to a summer camp in New Hampshire. When we got there, we met three brothers from Philadelphia. They were from the Burpee Seed Company family and were quickly nicknamed Big Burp, Little Burp, and Hiccup. My brothers and I were instantly nicknamed Big Butt, Little Butt, and Zipper. For years I was called Zipper. I later thought that was not Zippy enough for someone of my stylish, grand, holier-than-thou self, and when I went off to college, I just listed my name as Dick (now I am not sure if that was the best idea!). I hope you understand that I tell you this aside to keep us from being too serious, since this is a conversation, and conversations don't have to be academic works of art.

However, dear buddies, I do have to tell you that my love affair with skating, which began at an early age when the Zipper moniker applied, has been in zipping over a large expanse of ice, hearing music that fueled me (and still does), and the lifting, floating, soaring freedom that is possible. I also appreciated then—and even more now—

the romance of learning all the other creative parts that come with the Fine Art of Figure Skating.

Isn't that why we are all here together on this couch?

Figure skating is more than just a sport. Its essence spans the realms of music, design, performance, physical achievement, history, and emotion. While aspects of it may be measured, it will never be totally reduced to the level of measurement. Can anyone measure the expansion of your heart when love strikes?

So, let me ask all of you sharing the couch along with the dogs and me: where do we want to see skating go from here? Do we want to continue the journey we have already been taking? Wasn't it great that it was inspired by something as simple and as much fun as skating? Yet when we talk about our inspiration from the past, we have to hope none of us are killy-loo birds, which, according to Gustave Lussi, are birds that only fly backward because they aren't interested in where they are going, but where they have been. We have to look forward into the future to try and see what we have to do now to keep the Fine Art of Figure Skating modern but still rooted in the great values of its past.

Listen, guys, we all know from looking back that any love affair has changes that can swing back and forth like a pendulum. Skating, too, has had its changes. The discipline of figures doesn't exist anymore because it was not income-producing and not good television. (I can't tell you now many hours we spent daily learning them). The judging system desperately needed change, and got it with a new judging system (the IJS).

If we're going to look at where we go from here, let's first ask a few questions about *here*!

1. Do you like what you are seeing in skating today?

Personally, I don't like that I couldn't see the 2013 World Championships live on network television. That's probably because the ratings in the U.S. have dropped into the cellar where the doggies are sent when they are bad.

The 2014 World Skating Championships are held in March right after the big hoopla of the Olympic Winter Games and won't be seen live, except as a two-week delayed summary show in April.

2. Why has the popularity of skating dropped so much?

Since I seem to be the sponsor of this popcorn fest, let me start. It is my feeling that skating has lost its popularity because the new rules have made it incomprehensible to most of us groupies who are watching. (Since I no longer compete, commentate, or produce TV programs, I can call myself a groupie! Some call me a couch potato. I prefer being a groupie! Remember also, we groupies make up more of the audience than all the members of the USFS membership! Or used to!) Of course, the head honchos understand what's going on, but we lowlies seem befuddled by what the rules mean. Why don't we see a score of 6 anymore, and what the heck does a "personal best" of 208.36 points mean? Was it the skater's best score of the year? Or the skater's best for that particular program? Or the best of all the skater's programs during the competition? Or the best of the skater's entire career? I am sure everyone in Officialdom knows the answers, but the rest of us competing for space on the couch with the pooches don't have a clue, and why is it important, anyway?

Of course, the reason we don't see scores of 6 anymore is because the new judging system has instituted specific marks first for Technical Scores and then for Program Component Scores (remember the chapter on the IJS?). These are all measurements, as I have said, of every little thing someone can think of to be marked. It was supposed to stop the rampant cheating that had been going on, which culminated in the 2002 Scandal of Salt Lake City.

3. Did it stop the cheating?

No! A Ukrainian judge was suspended this year for

cheating, and many have told me there is a little "winky winky" going on in the Program Component Scores. But the new rules certainly made everything confusing—for example, how could a skater fall twice and get a 10? And they also make everything secret—for example, who gave that 10? So, for those of us on the couch who are attempting to be logical despite the beer we've consumed, the next logical question is:

4. Did secrecy help stop the cheating?

Will someone please pass the mixed nuts? We need to fortify ourselves for this nutty situation.

To answer this question, there is a report titled, "Does Transparency Reduce Favoritism and Corruption? Evidence from the Reform of Figure Skating Judging" It is by Eric Zitzewitz, published by the National Bureau of Economic Research (#17732 January 2012).

The report concludes:

"Transparency is usually thought to reduce favoritism and corruption by facilitating monitoring by outsiders, but there is concern it can have the perverse effect of facilitating collusion by insiders. In response to vote trading scandals . . . , the . . . ISU introduced a number of changes to its judging system, including obscuring which judge issued which mark. The stated intent was to disrupt collusion by groups of judges, but this change also frustrates most attempts by outsiders to monitor judge behavior. I [the author] find that the 'compatriot-judge effect', which aggregates favoritism (nationalistic bias from own-country judges) and corruption (vote trading), actually increased slightly after the reforms."

This guy certainly makes valid points.

5. So, if we still have cheating, what was the purpose of the new scoring system?

By assigning points to everything, it was intended to make it difficult for judges to "bend" the scores to the result they might want. This was happily called "absolute judging."

The new system assigned marks, levels, grades of execution, and criteria to all and sundry movements that could possibly appear in a figure skating program. It was frankly intended to push the level of difficulty, to make the competition more difficult—just as a speed skater has to skate faster and faster in order to set a new record. It was intended to make competition more technical and to hell with musicality, passion, performance, and all those wonderful things that make up creativity. It was a speed skater's vision to make figure skating a gymnastic-type sport where the number of revolutions, different positions in spins, and all sorts of flying body parts must be included and can be counted, thus eliminating reliance on subjective opinions.

So we have to ask (even though the dogs are barking to go out) whether the next question must be . . .

6. **Has this system helped increase the level of enjoyment of those of us who watch figure skating?**

Guess what? I say no. I don't like seeing cookie-cutter programs that repeat the same choreography, including multiple falls and multiple spins that seem to be drunken, and endless repetitive arm movements worming everywhere. (A bit snarky, you say? Well, yes. But then, if you've been paying attention to this conversation, what else did you expect me to say?)

7. **So, what's to be done?**

SPLIT THE ISU INTO TWO SEPARATE FEDERATIONS!

Get wise, figure skaters, and take back control!

Speed skaters should not govern figure skating! Figure skaters should govern themselves, and create their own rules. This is not a place for the multi-headed Hydra of Greek mythology to operate.

Somehow I doubt that many countries will stand up and support such a radical idea, even though if the U.S., Canada, Great Britain, and some others did, there would be action. Change is not exactly figure skating's middle name. It took over half a century for figures to be eliminated (a really major action for this constipated, stuffy, conservative, frozen, world of figure skating to accomplish).

Yet this split is possible. It will take time. The present president of the USFS is due to finish her post in the spring of 2014. A position on the ISU Council is a place where one can continue one's connections with skating and retain the perks of travel and importance. That position is most likely available only to someone who agrees with everything Ottavio Cinquanta, the current president of the ISU, wants. Therefore, any support by the United States for such a radical idea is probably minimal for the time being.

Only if figure skating declines into enough of a financial mess to force change will this split occur. That may already be happening. The ISU has reduced the number of official meetings, the amount of time various ISU officials can attend at an event, the number of seminars, the amount of reimbursement of board and lodging for the skaters, and the number of days a judge can stay at an event, and there is no TV contract in place at this time for American network exposure, which in the past was a chief area of income! Even if it is announced that NBC or any other network will pick up a U.S. TV package, I am sure there will be no generous guarantee; only a share of possible profits.

Remember there is total secrecy about the finances of the ISU! United States Figure Skating (USFS) is a 501(c)(3) organization and therefore a non-profit organization (which makes donations tax-deductible), yet it is heavily affected by decisions of the ISU, which is a secretive organization! Shouldn't this be changed? A little transparency, please!

Another reason a split is needed is because there are over eighty Federations within the ISU, and more are constantly being added, particularly in smaller countries that in many cases have little skating (Grenada and Cyprus), yet all of which have equal votes with countries that have substantial figure skating activity like Japan, the U.S., and Canada!

But the most significant point and the true idiocy of this is that not only do the speed skating Federations get a substantial part of their income from figure skating (which means less income for figure skating), but their delegates also vote on the rules for figure skating (the IJS). Many speed skaters, including ISU president Ottavio Cinquanta (who has stated it), know little if anything about figure skating and couldn't care less about it. Nevertheless, the speed skating Federations voted on the International Judging System (the IJS), which are the figure skating rules that OC (as we sometimes call him) presented to the ISU Congress and which now govern figure skating!

Let's face the fact that figure skating has a leader *who is a speed skater*. We have a leader who may be charming and personable but may not comprehend the Fine Art of Figure Skating and its dual principles of technical merit and artistic impression. Remember, there has not been an ISU president who was a figure skater in more than thirty-five years. OC was elected president twelve years before the 2002 Scandal of Salt Lake City. When faced with the 2002 Scandal of Salt Lake City and the need to create a new judging system, OC made secrecy the name of the game. His primary goal was to prevent further scandals. Now, more than a decade after the scandal, he still has not recognized, nor may not wish to recognize, that while there were major problems in both the old and new judging systems, there are good points in both systems. The world of figure skating now needs someone who is capable of combining the two systems and taking the best of both.

For someone to admit they may have made some mistakes may be difficult, but it is a mark of great leadership. OC should not squander this opportunity to accomplish the necessary ultimate reform and leave a legacy of being a great leader of this sport.

Any new leadership in the ISU will not happen quickly. The next election for ISU president is not until 2016. It should have been in 2014. At the ISU Congress, which met in 2012 in Kuala Lumpur, Ottavio Cinquanta introduced Resolution 7 in order to extend the terms of all the ISU officeholders. It was a move to abort the constitution of the ISU and was made because Ottavio Cinquanta was age ineligible to run for another term. The majority of the voters were from the speed skating camp who received much of their income from figure skating and were happy to oblige. Thus he was able (and they, too) to retain the perks and the pay resulting from his position as president. Also included was the ability to fund still more Federations in minor countries that had little figure skating but could be counted on to agree to OC's requests.

(As an aside, OC announced he was "stepping down" in 2016! He had already aborted the constitution once, and to try to abort it again was probably difficult, so he just very nicely (?) announced it as "stepping down." He also announced that a new history of the ISU would be published at that time. I can just see the aura of holiness that will surround that book and the characters in it!)

The difficult part of this Resolution 7 is that the next President, whoever that may be, will have only two years before the next Olympics in 2018, so that means little change can be implemented before still another cycle of the Olympic Winter Games (2022) comes around.

Remember, I am no longer a competitor, and I am not now, nor will I ever, run for office in either the USFS or the ISU. No one would vote for me anyway, and I am older than Methuselah and therefore can say what I want. And I do! Just try not to smear me with the catsup I see you putting on your hot dog!

I remind you (again), there has been no figure skater as

president of the ISU for more than forty years! I can assure you the politics will be roiling leading up to that time in 2016, with political maneuvering not only by the new potential leaders but by the old as well. The same will also happen two years later, when there is another election. Let's just hope someone will be elected who is not a speed skater and does not have a speed skating vision.

The Fine Art of Figure Skating cannot and should not be totally submerged in a morass of measurement and secrecy. I hope to see it rebuild the qualities of emotion, personality, flow, clarity, grace, and elegant calmness that too often seem to have eluded it. It will take a rethinking of the artistic, creative side of the sport and making the Program Component Scores truly equal in importance to the Technical Scores (they may be mathematically, but not in reality). It will take a new set of rules that don't measure every little tweety tooting hiccup that occurs. It will take a reduction in the number of rule amendments and instructions that arrive by e-mail on too many Thursday nights and are scheduled to take effect the following Mondays. It will also take an increase in the level of respect for judges, despite the fact that there may have been some really bad apples in that basket.

Most important, it will have to stop rewarding failure by giving high marks to jumps that are missed!
Again, there are both good and bad points in the old and the new judging systems. A sensitive hand is needed to combine the best of both.

(I have been lusting for one of my asides, and this time there will be an aside within an aside!) As a very young skater, I was given ice dance lessons. In those days, that meant doing specific ballroom dances on ice: the Foxtrot, Waltz, Tango, Quickstep, Blues, and the Kilian. I did not like ice dancing because I felt constricted by the tight patterns and precise steps that were all laid out in a Rulebook and which had to be followed exactly. Although I passed most of my tests, I was at heart a free skater. I was like a young kid who gets on a horse and just wants to ride off into the sunset. Forget about dressage and elegant riding, let alone precise, carefully prescribed and performed dances like a waltz or quickstep.

I got a reputation for disliking ice dancing.

But then the Fine Art of Ice Dancing changed, and I changed with it. From not being enthusiastic about ice dancing as a youngster, I have come to feel it can be innovative, inspiring, and creative. Single and pair skaters are immersed in jumps and jump combinations, spending too much time stuffing their program full of dippy-doodle moves whose only reason for being is to garner points.

And now for the aside within the aside! Occasionally I give lectures about my garden and how skating influenced it. I talk about the relationship between a straight line step in skating and the straight borders in my garden at Ice Pond Farm.

The straight line step has historically been a step sequence that moves in one direction from one end of the rink to the other. The hockey barriers are the straight line enclosures. The step is actually anything but straight. The rules require the skater to "busy it up," lunging forward, backward, doing inside and outside edges, kicks, turns, dips, toe runs, changes of edges, slides, loops, brackets, rockers, knee bends, and all sorts of leg kicks.

In my garden, the hedges of the borders are like the straight line enclosures of the hockey barriers. But within that enclosure, I let the plants go wild in an extravagant whoop-de-do. In the lecture I show film of Evan Lysacek doing a straight-line sequence that is a masterpiece of movement and a smashing display of steps reminiscent of a careening rudderless sailboat caught in a whirlpool. In the garden, it shows up as the massing and messing of all sorts of flowering plants, tall and short, round and pointed, fat and skinny, in all sorts of colors—which can overpower your senses, particularly in autumn, when the plants go crazy. For me at least, it is an interesting comparison.

But the issue here is that this jumble of movement is not more than an exclamation point in the much larger landscape of Ice Pond Farm—and similarly, the jumble of body movements in a straight line step should only be one small piece of a skating program and should not be in every part of the program, like the frenetic arm movements we see from start to finish. Spins should not have to change positions so that we have no time to register and appreciate whether they are at least centered and whether the positions add to the story the skater is telling. Can you imagine if the whole landscape were such a busy, raging jungle of hysteria?

This is why I feel ice dancers today seem to have a corner on the market of the entertainment value of skating.

The work of Torvill and Dean (T and D), Moiseyeva and Minenkov, Blumberg and Seibert, and so many others has led the way to today's world of ice dancing and ultimately to current stars like Davis and White.

How could this be, when the rules for ice dancing also are over the top?

The Rules state that the music for ice dancing must be: "suitable for Ice Dance as a sport discipline" (what does that mean?).

In addition:

"i) The music must have an audible rhythmic beat and melody, or audible rhythmic beat alone, but not melody alone, and may be vocal. The music may be without an audible rhythmic beat for up to 10 seconds at the beginning or end of the program and up to 10 seconds during the program."

(That is a no-no, whatever "that" is. Just remember the fuss and feathers over T and D's *Bolero*.)
And:

"ii) The music must have at least one change of tempo <u>and</u> expression. These changes may be gradual or immediate, but in either case they must be obvious."

(Just make sure it is obvious and you will be OK!)

But wait! There's more:

"iii) All music including classical music must be cut/edited, orchestrated or arranged in a way that it creates an interesting, colorful, entertaining dance program with different dance moves for a building effect."

(That's good to hear.)

Now, beat with me and bear with me for a bit more (did I say that?):

"iv) The music must be suitable for the Couple's skating skills and technical ability."

(Does that mean if you are not very good, you should use music that is not very good?)

And finally: "Free Dance music that does not adhere to these requirements will be penalized by a deduction (see Rule 353, paragraph 1.n) (ii))."

Are we finished? My goodness! Much of this is the result of T and D's seismic change in the vision of ice dancing.

At the 2010 National Championships, ice dancers Meryl Davis and Charlie White skated to music from *The Phantom of the Opera*. The music, with its sweeping melodic lines and emotion-driven story, was a good choice for their skating style. It had been used many times by others, all of whom were disadvantaged by the necessity of fitting endless moves, jump combinations, dance steps, and swinging, bending, and whipsawing arms that looked like an egg beater on high voltage!

It was the passion and the musicality that marked the performance of Davis and White and allowed them to override the complexity and the silliness of the ice dance rules. Davis and White were lacking in physical similarity. He looked the part of an all-American footballer, with long, wildly flowing blond hair. She was the tiny, dark, meticulously put together, perfectly arranged contrast. It was already a statement of black and white, high and low, ever-moving, contrasting elements.

They captured the eye of this beholder! But more than their appearance, it was their commitment to the emotional content of the music and their total and honest passion that caught and held attention. They were also blessed with brilliant choreography by Igor Shpilband and Marina Zueva that gave them the framework for the picture they created, which both entertained and excited the audience.

Compare this to Mao Asada's performance in the ladies' competition at the recent 2013 World Championships in London, Ontario. She skated to *Swan Lake*. The costume had white feathers. The jumps were excellent. But to repeat, *Swan Lake* comes with a hundred years of history.

That history and music are imbued with the body language of swans, their sinuous movements and the perfection of their arching, stretching positions. When we see swans on a lake even without the famous music, we can't help but see the magic of their physicality. One hundred years of dance performances highlights and honors this. Asada didn't embrace that or give an honest commitment to what is the essence of *Swan Lake*. (I trust that all of us figure skaters have seen dancers perform *Swan Lake* and understand what the heck I am talking about: the extreme position, the stretch, the arch, the lightness of touch, and the exquisite posture. But from a speed skater's perspective, capturing the essence of swans' movements would not be of value in winning a race (let alone this "sport" of figure skating).

Anyone taking on a role in *Swan Lake* must deliver more than just compliance with the rules and the necessity of filling every second with movement—which is the exact opposite of what the swans do with their slow progression across the lake. Make note of the way Oksana Baiul skated to *Swan Lake* at the 1994 Olympic Winter Games in Lillehammer. She became a swan in that performance— but that also was before the IJS went into play and there was still room for judges to vote their opinions, even if it did include a little block judging.

Yuna Kim is blessed with two talents that will stand her in good stead at the forthcoming Olympic Winter Games in Sochi. Her jumps are simply the best. They're clean, easy, and consistent, with height, excellent rotation, and perfect entrances and exits.

She also has the ability "Not to Wilt" (see chapter 9), and these two positives should help her in her quest to medal at Sochi.

Her arm movements are graceful and she skates to the music, but the emotion seems applied and to be created as an effect instead of coming from the heart. Her expression can take on a suffering look. What is it they say about the figures in a Titian painting? "If the heroine is a dancer, it's a Degas. If the heroine is suffering, it's a Titian."

This may be heresy in some folks' minds, since Yuna Kim has gotten the highest of scores under the IJS, but next time you see her skate, observe her back. She has rounded shoulders that lack tension. She fails to ever fully point or turn out her feet, so that in a spiral or a spin one sees feet that look like wooden mallets. She is incredibly bright about her skating, and if she reads this before the Olympics, I am sure you will see improvement in these two problem areas.

I will remember her performance in future years for the jumps, which again are light, elegant, steady, clean and truly marvelous. I suspect I will not remember her program for the total concept. She has not yet achieved, in my humble opinion, that requirement for greatness of leaving the sport different and better just because she was in it. (Remember my earlier statement that my criticisms are made for the talented!) For me, the sport is neither different nor better just because there were very good jumps in it.

In the 1956 National Championships in Philadelphia,

Carol Heiss, Cathy Machado and Tenley Albright each skated programs that were different in concept, choreography, and feeling from each other. They also were entertaining and kept us enthralled (now, don't tell me that was half a century ago and there were no triples or triple combinations in them! I know. Keeping an audience enthralled isn't only about the number of revolutions a body can do in the air.).

T and D's *Bolero*, John Curry's *Don Quixote*, the Protopopovs' *Swan Lake*, Brian Boitano's 1988 Olympic performance, Janet Lynn's *Prelude to the Afternoon of a Faun*, and Tenley Albright's *Graduation Ball* were all memorable and left the Fine Art of Figure Skating better. Is the sport of figure skating better because Denise Beillmann popularized the catchfoot? It is certainly more fun and more dazzling, but is it *better*? It certainly did not become better just because I did the first triple jump.

What do I think made skating better? Here are some things I'll remember. I will remember the edging of Dorothy Hamill as she showed us the meaning of position. I will remember the lift and floating quality in delayed Axels, and the stretch, pointed feet, and the elegance of Belita Jepson-Turner in the movie *Suspense*, and the lessons in grace, beauty, fire, personality, and clarity of so many others I've mentioned and not mentioned in this conversation.

In my long-standing observation, what registers for me is the quality of the skating itself, the human emotion, the impact, and the overall creative concept that brings together all the arts that are possible in the Fine Art of Figure Skating.

A tall order? Why not? Just ask for some caviar with your champagne!

Figure skating always has great popularity where there are champions and where those champions have personality that makes them "stars." America has had them, and so has Russia. Great Britain had its time, too.

And now Japan and Korea have their moment. There are some who have been at the top for quite a while and are likely to retire soon, like Russia's Evgeni Plushenko and France's Brian Joubert. Italy has Carolina Kostner. But how about England? Austria?

Anytime there is an outstanding, impactful figure skater in a country, there will be excitement and more who will emerge, like Robin Cousins after John Curry, the succession of American skating ladies (Dorothy after Peggy; Sarah and Tara after Kristi, and of course the Russian contingent, Gordeeva/Grinkov after Rodnina/Zaitsev after the Protopopovs, and the many dance couples one after the other. Incidentally, that juggernaut mostly disappeared soon after the Soviet Union dissolved and stopped sponsoring the sport).

Too many young skaters in the U.S. do not want to compete. Yes, the sport is vibrant in synchronized skating, which is an invigorating, very pleasant activity for young skaters who learn to skate in unison. Most likely they won't learn to do many quadruples. Are we doing enough to incubate artistry, personality, and pizzazz in the figure skating stars of tomorrow? It is these star competitors who inspire more young skaters.

So, what's my wish list for where we go from here?

In addition to splitting the figure and speed skating Federations, I would hope that there would be new rules that would still allow for two programs, but programs that are quite different in intent. The first would be a technically oriented program that, like the Short Program, would emphasize measurement but still include artistry. Any time limit should be generously wide. The second program would be one where artistry is more important than the technical (measured) marks. The two programs would thus not have the same cause to be so deadly similar in choreography, and differentiating between them would allow for the creative force, the theatricality that is inherent in skating, to take a more prominent place.

The next item on my wish list (needed in order to achieve this) is:

Greater respect for judges.

This is the difficult area. Most judges are honest individuals, particularly if they are not subjugated by their Federations. But like judges in the rest of our world, they need to be not only educated but also controlled. Could that entail making panels of permanent judges who are not only educated in the nuances of skating but who are also free of their Federations' influence, if they ever could be?

Now that would be a major change.

Let's all hope to see this world of skating return to sanity, and a day when endless frantic movement will no longer cloud the whole picture. This is not to say that fast, complicated step sequences and frantic movement can't be valuable, but intelligent choreography should be able to incorporate that as part of the picture the skater is painting, not in response to still another rule. What we don't need are rules that advocate endless movements that have no lasting significance and demand shallow bits of ornament. The flailing of arms like so many forkfuls of limp spaghetti and the tilting of a skaters head to signify serious emotion should not be rewarded. An honest presentation can outrank the excesses that have reached a peak in programs. Ornament is ok, but only if it supports the intent of the program. It can even be extravagant if its objectives are clear and it's done with quality and panache. I guess I'm saying that we should strive to make figure skating and the system for judging it clearer and more rewarding.

Let me ask again, wouldn't it be great if everything were as simple as ice-skating? (Correction! It is not simple; it just seems that way because it began with nothing more than a pair of blades and some ice, and because it has taught our body, given us joy, taught us the meaning of passion, and also the ability to change our mind and our direction—and isn't that enough?)

Did you ever expect something so profound to start from skating outdoors on a pond? I certainly didn't, bopping around on the ice in my Zipper years. But what an education skating gave me! The ongoing impact of learning to "see," the opportunity (and the interest) to follow other enthusiasms, the ability and willingness to be passionate about them—that is what the journey should be about. Perhaps, more than anything, the journey is the process of learning, of opening your mind and heart and embracing the notion that you are capable of changing your opinions, your mind, and your directions, also!

If you have ever been caught in the maelstrom that erupts when you are gripped by an enthusiasm, you have been blessed with a gift. If you allow it, you will find it spreads far and wide and takes you places you never thought possible. Its people and its history enrich and influence you; it leads you to new areas of interest. Most importantly, it expands your perceptions and most importantly your ability to *see*.

A good friend of mine once said that we live in a world where people often dress ugly, talk ugly, and build ugly. We have the power to correct this in our own individual worlds. Skating gives us the opportunity to express and experience beauty. It's a sport where beauty coexists with technical accomplishment. That combination has always fascinated us, challenged us, and sometimes eluded us. I hope we can find new ways to appreciate and reward skaters who awe and delight us!

Figure skating has been wonderful to me. I have made friends of lifelong standing and have had the pleasure of seeing many extraordinary performances. My eye has beheld so much, and my mind has registered marvels of every kind, from athletic valor and prowess to creative genius.

I am certain that skating, no matter what form it takes, will last. That is because it has a great sense of movement, it embraces music and design and humor, it supports competition both against ourselves as well as others, and it's still the only sport that anyone can do outdoors in a city in the winter. All you need is a pair of skates and a decent patch of ice. You don't have to be an Olympic competitor to enjoy the delights of skating.

So there will be, let's hope, many more times when we can get together on this creaky couch with the dogs. I have a sneaking feeling we will meet here again in the very near future, when we will continue to kvetch, complain, observe, applaud, criticize, and eat and drink too much.

But we will also continue to have one hell of a good time!

Thanks for coming!

ABOUT THE AUTHOR

Dick Button is widely considered one of the premier male figure skaters of all time. He dominated the world of figure skating for a seven-year period, winning two Olympic gold medals (1948 and 1952), five consecutive World Championships, and seven U.S. National titles. Button has since had a long and illustrious broadcasting career, and he became the first winner of an Emmy Award for "Outstanding Sports Personality – Analyst" in 1981. Button is a member of the World Figure Skating Hall of Fame and Olympic Hall of Fame. He is a graduate of Harvard College, Harvard Law School, and is a frequent garden lecturer. He has two children, Edward and Emily.

CPSIA information can be o
Printed in the USA
LVOW06s2120180314

377996LV00016B/572/P

9 781494 223472